Welcome

In this book you will find 35 unique illustrations of beautiful native American women proud of their origin and culture. Portaits are surrounded by relaxing mandala patterns. Each page is single sided to prevent from bleeding through to the next page.

I created this coloring book especially for you, so I hope you will enjoy.

Have fun!

David Locatello

This coloring book belongs to:

....

....

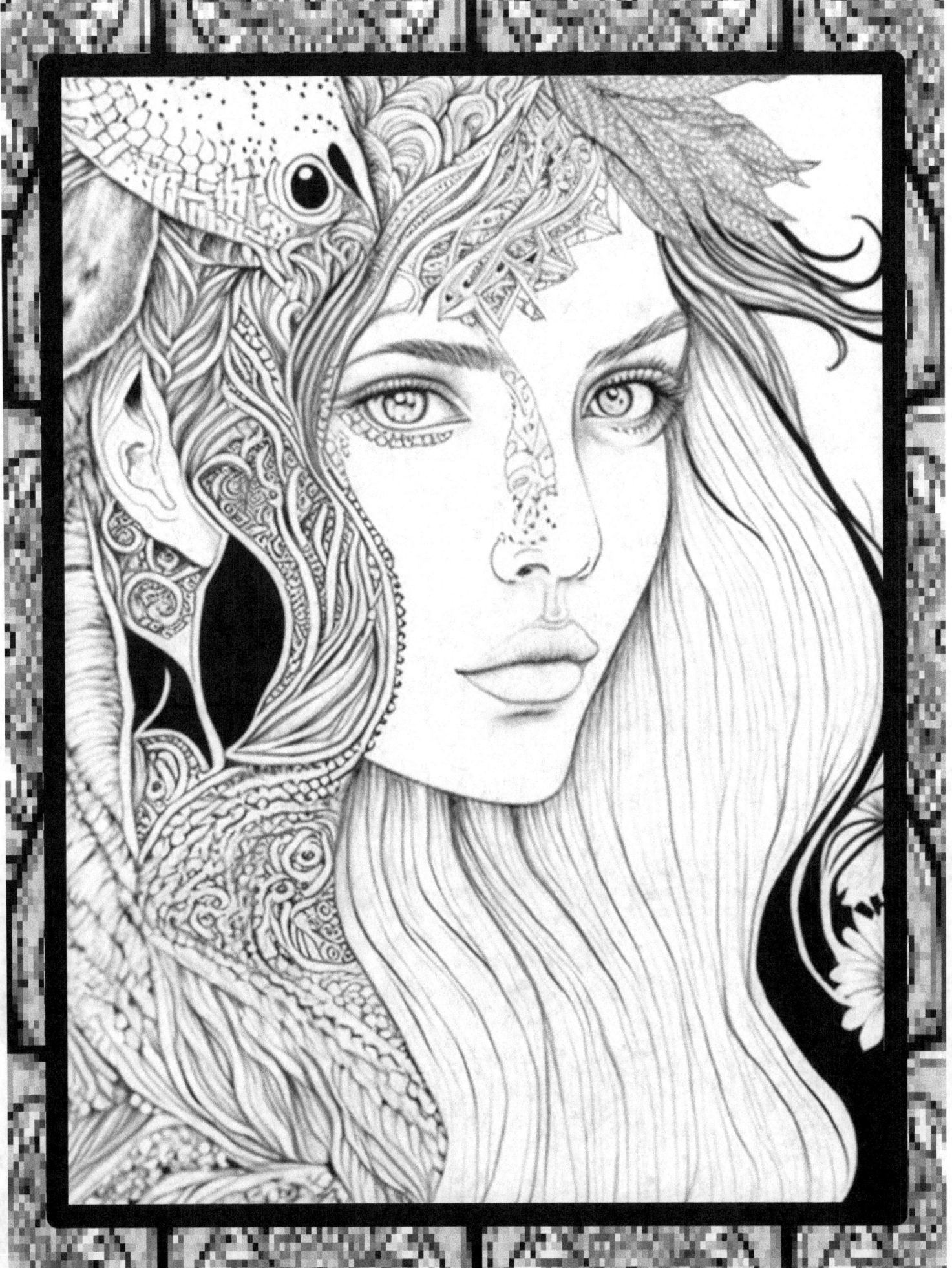

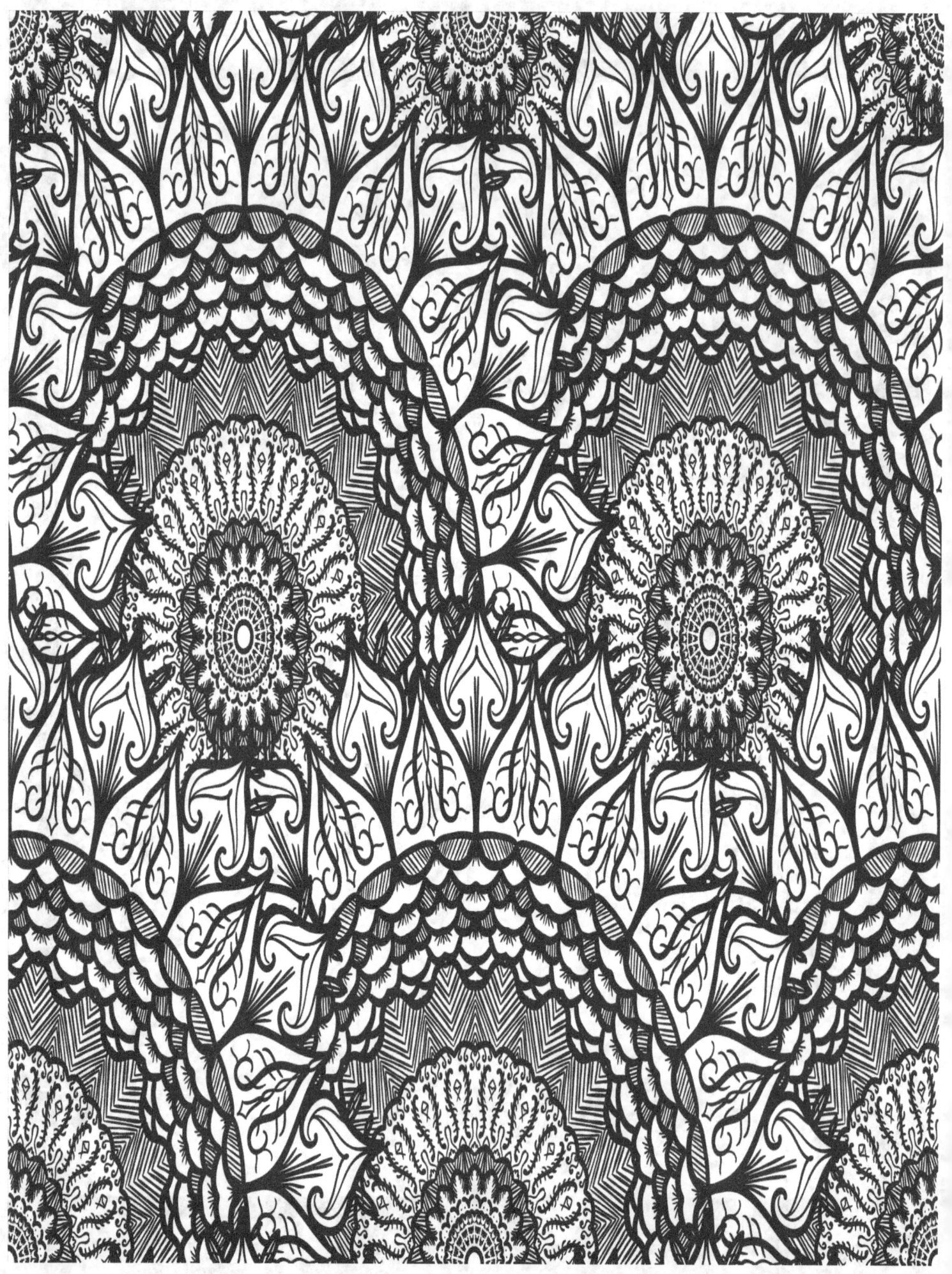

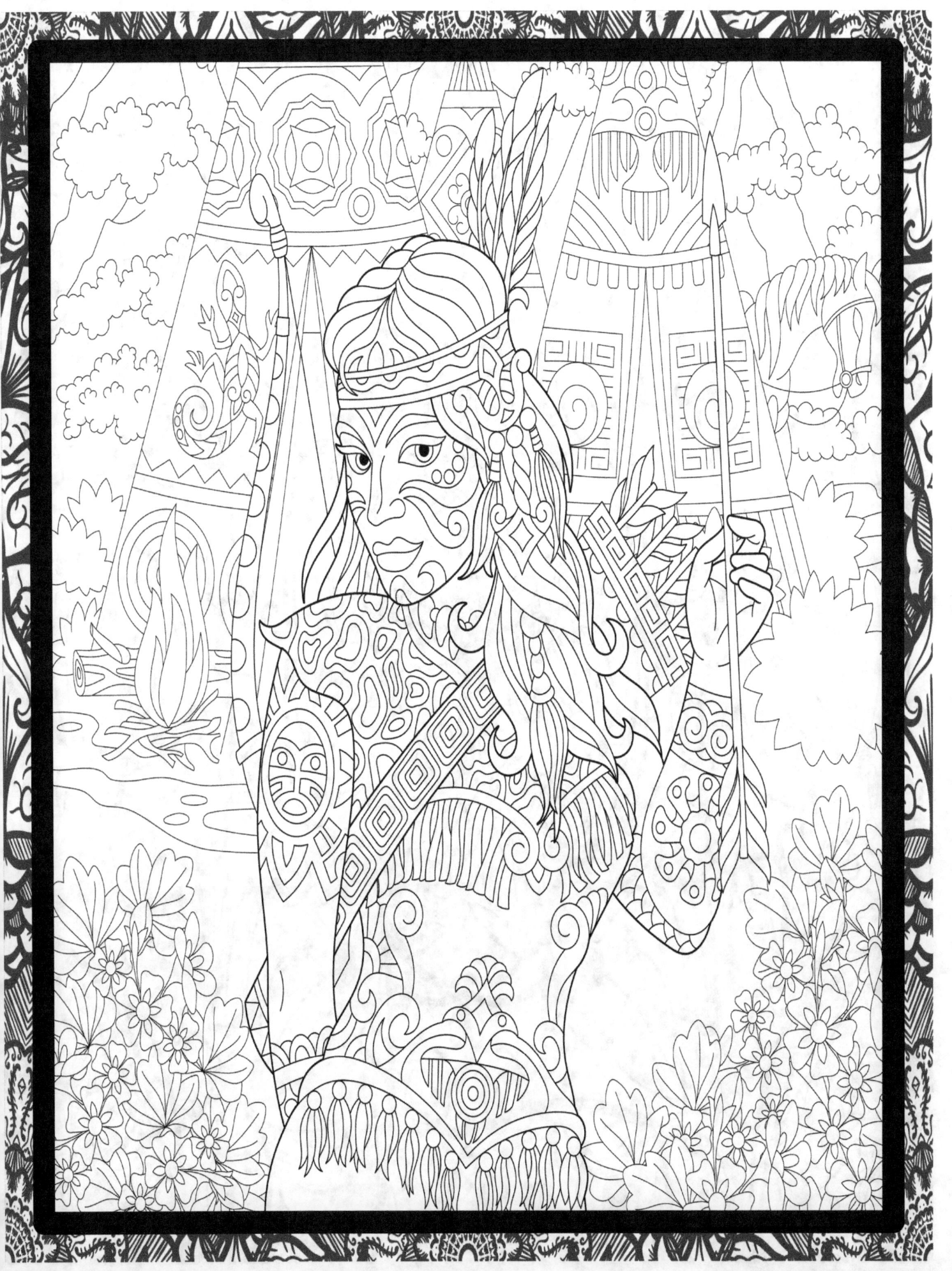

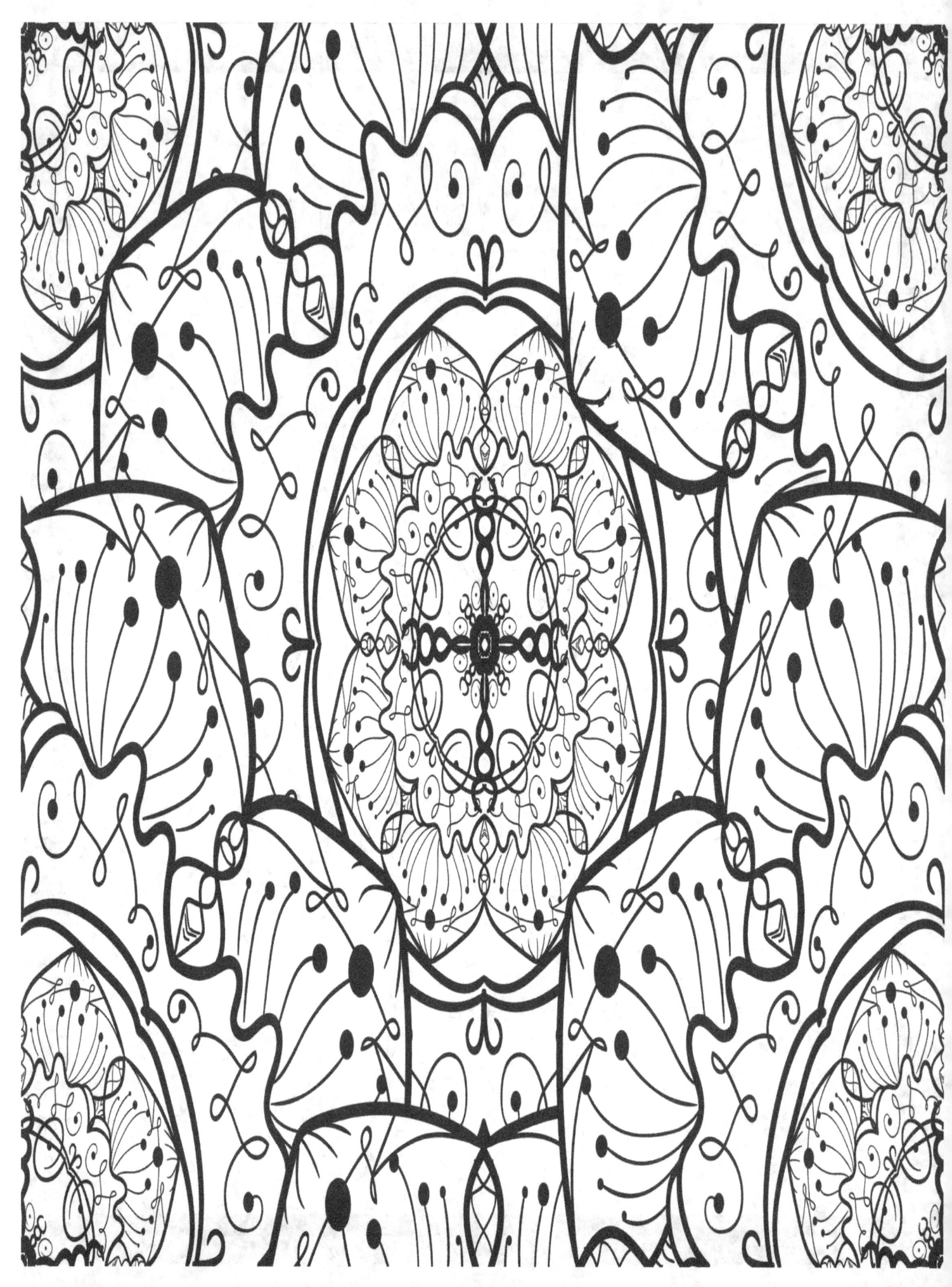

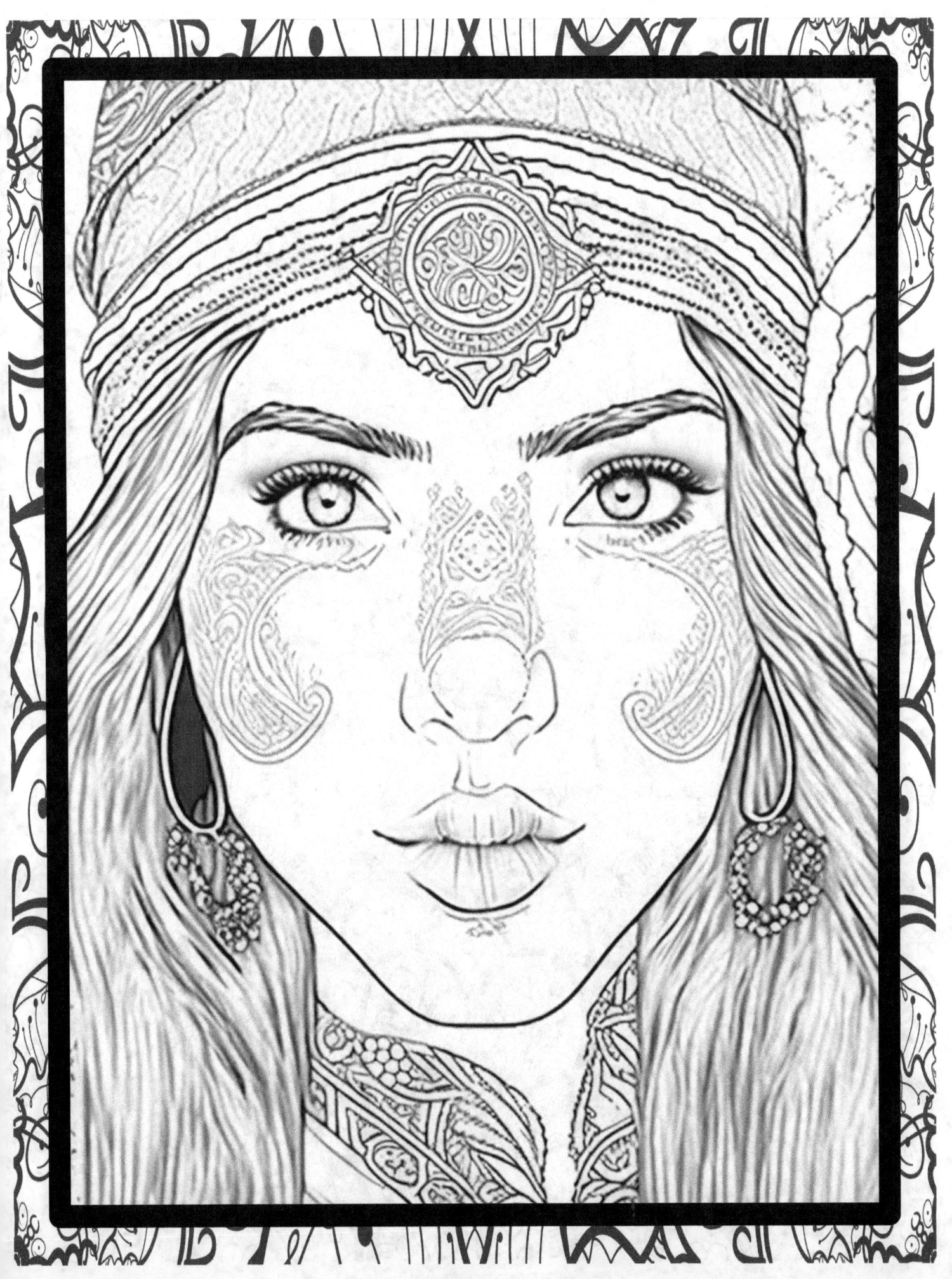

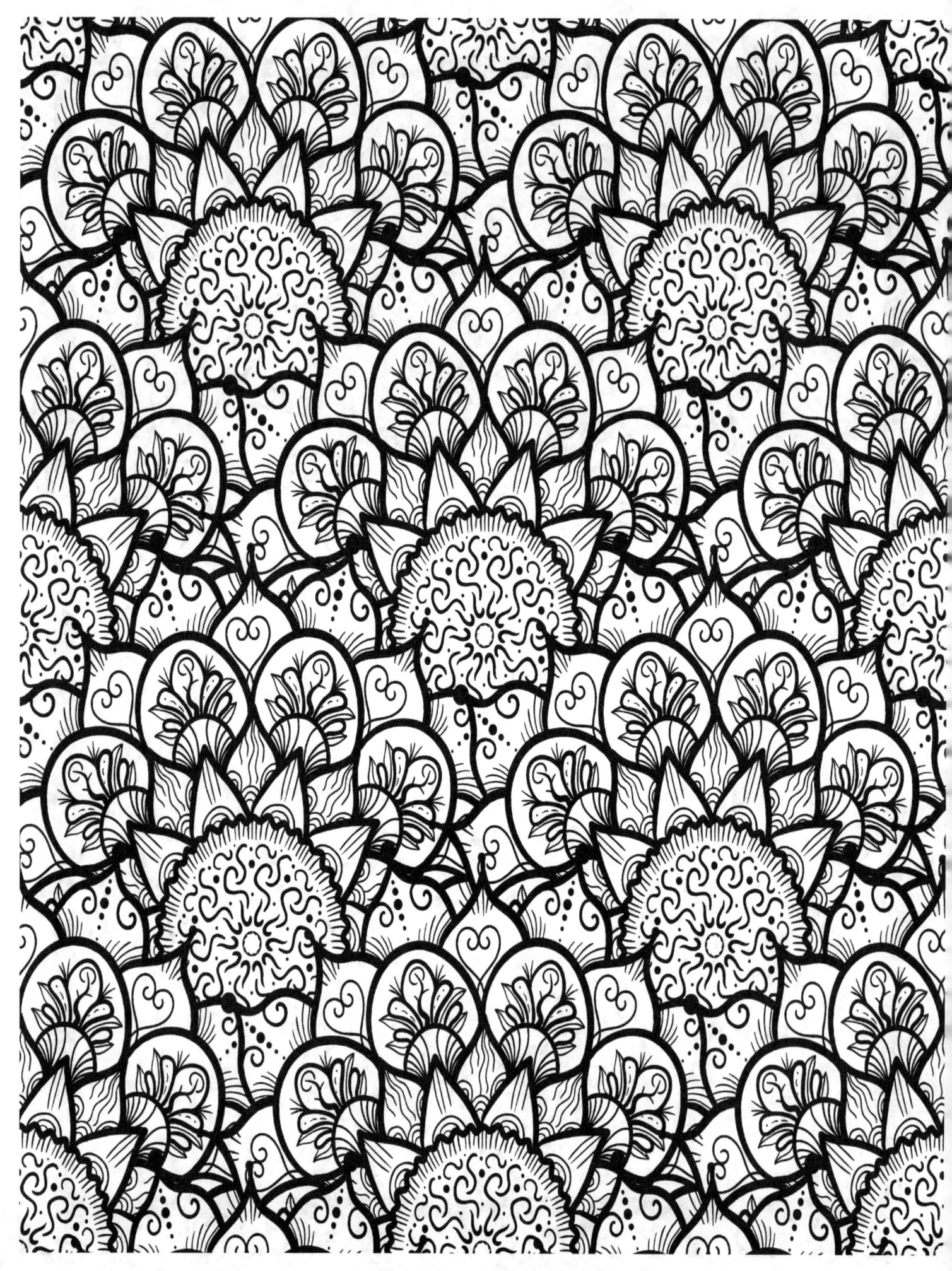

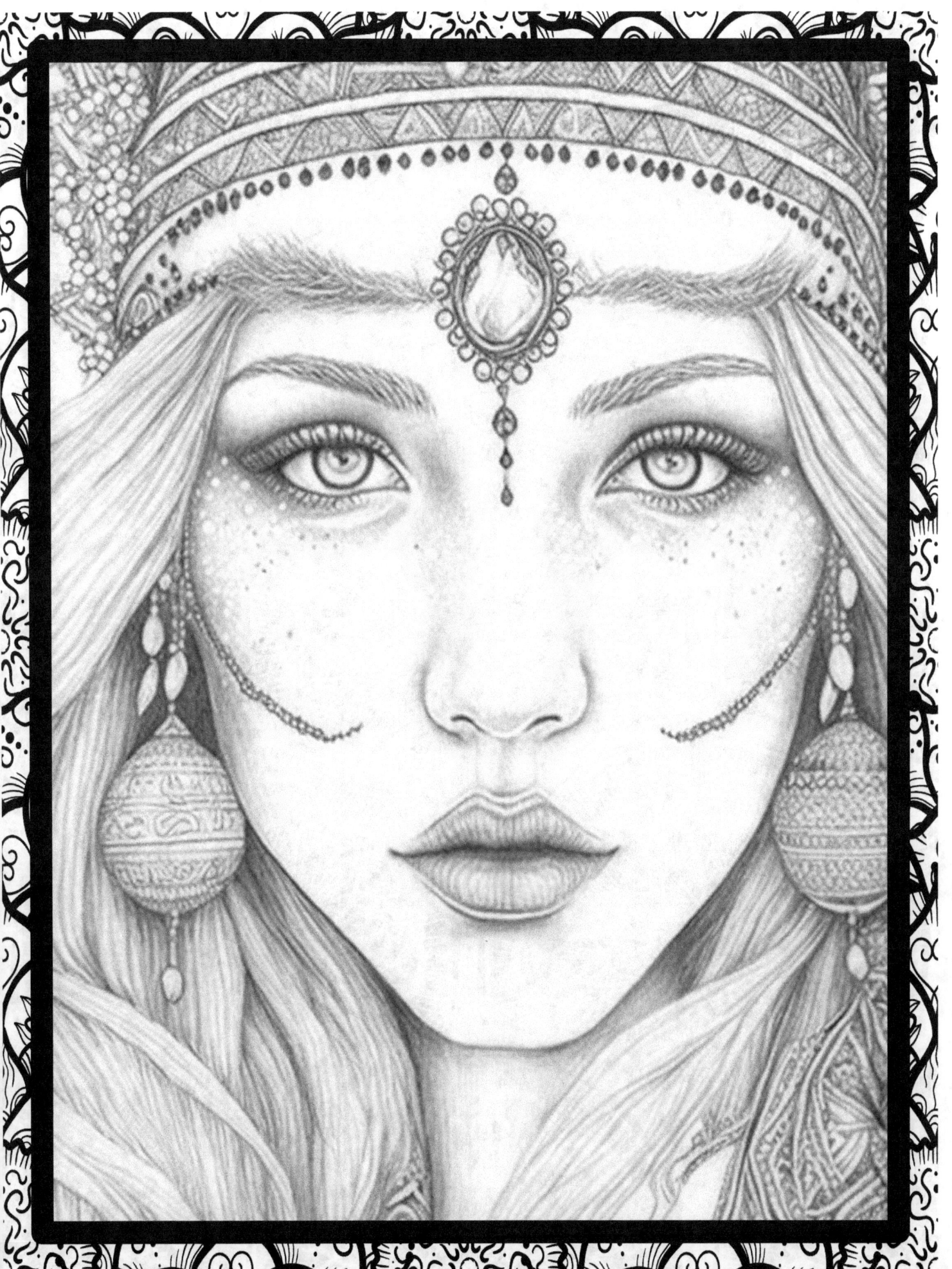

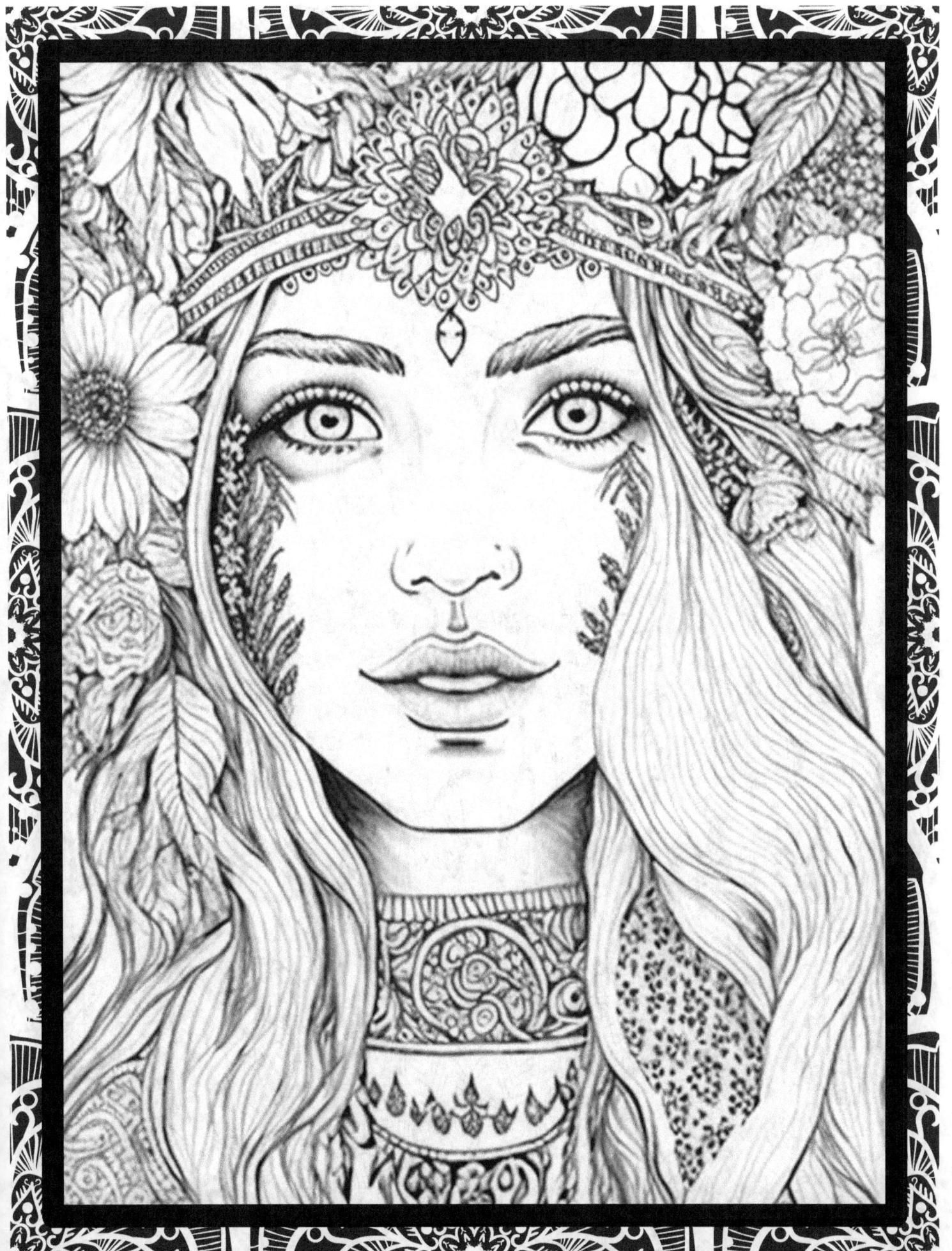

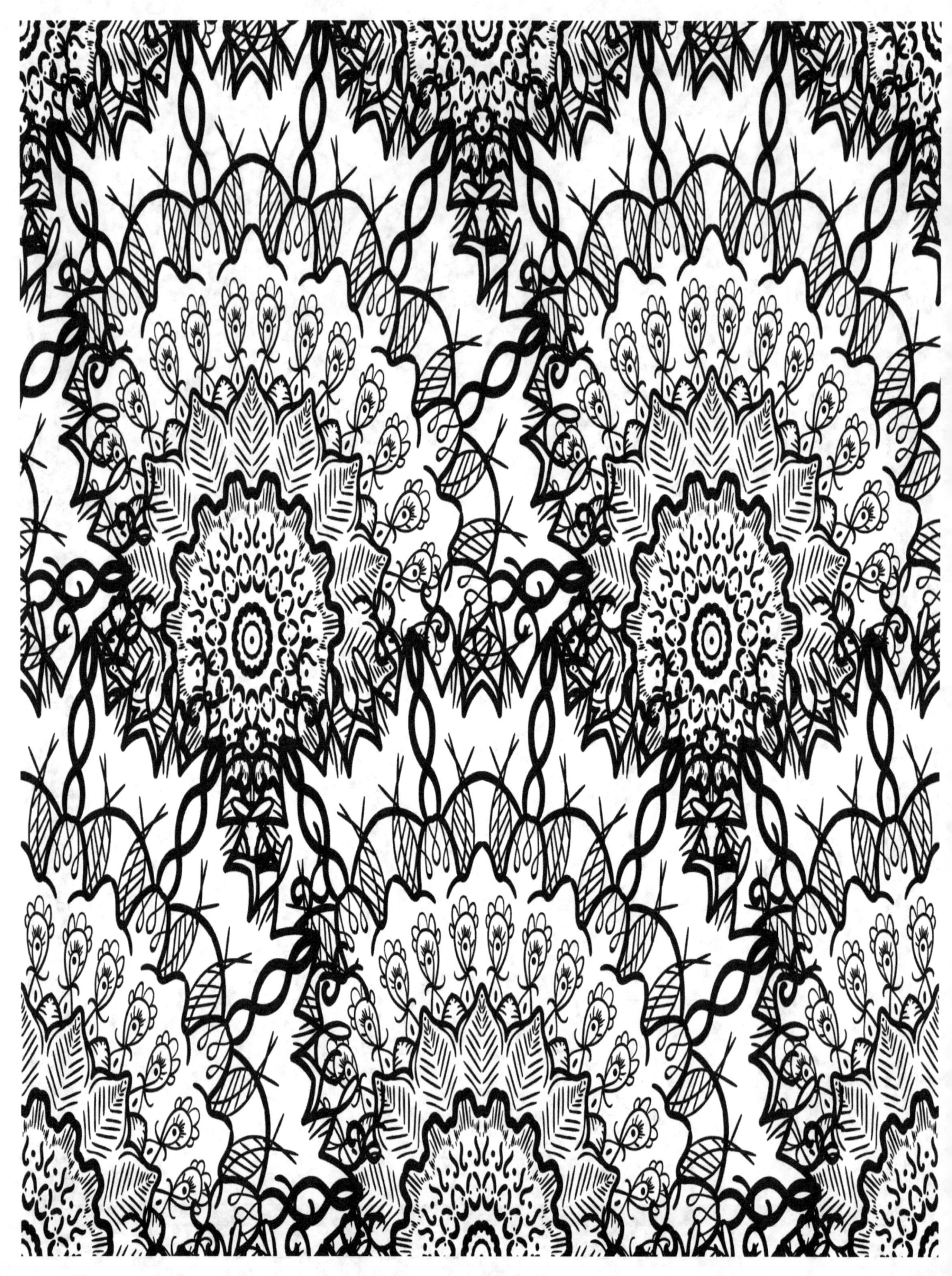

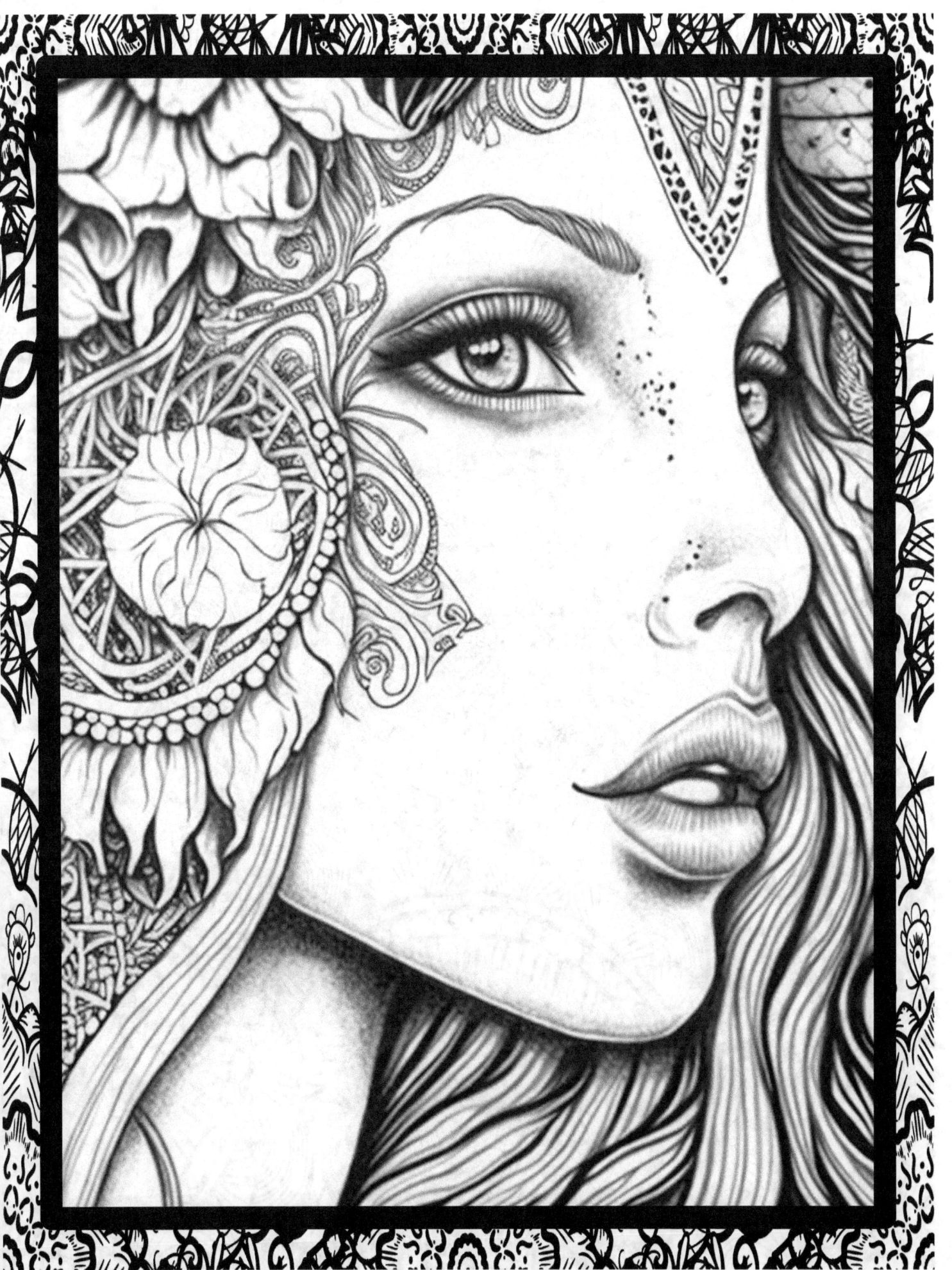

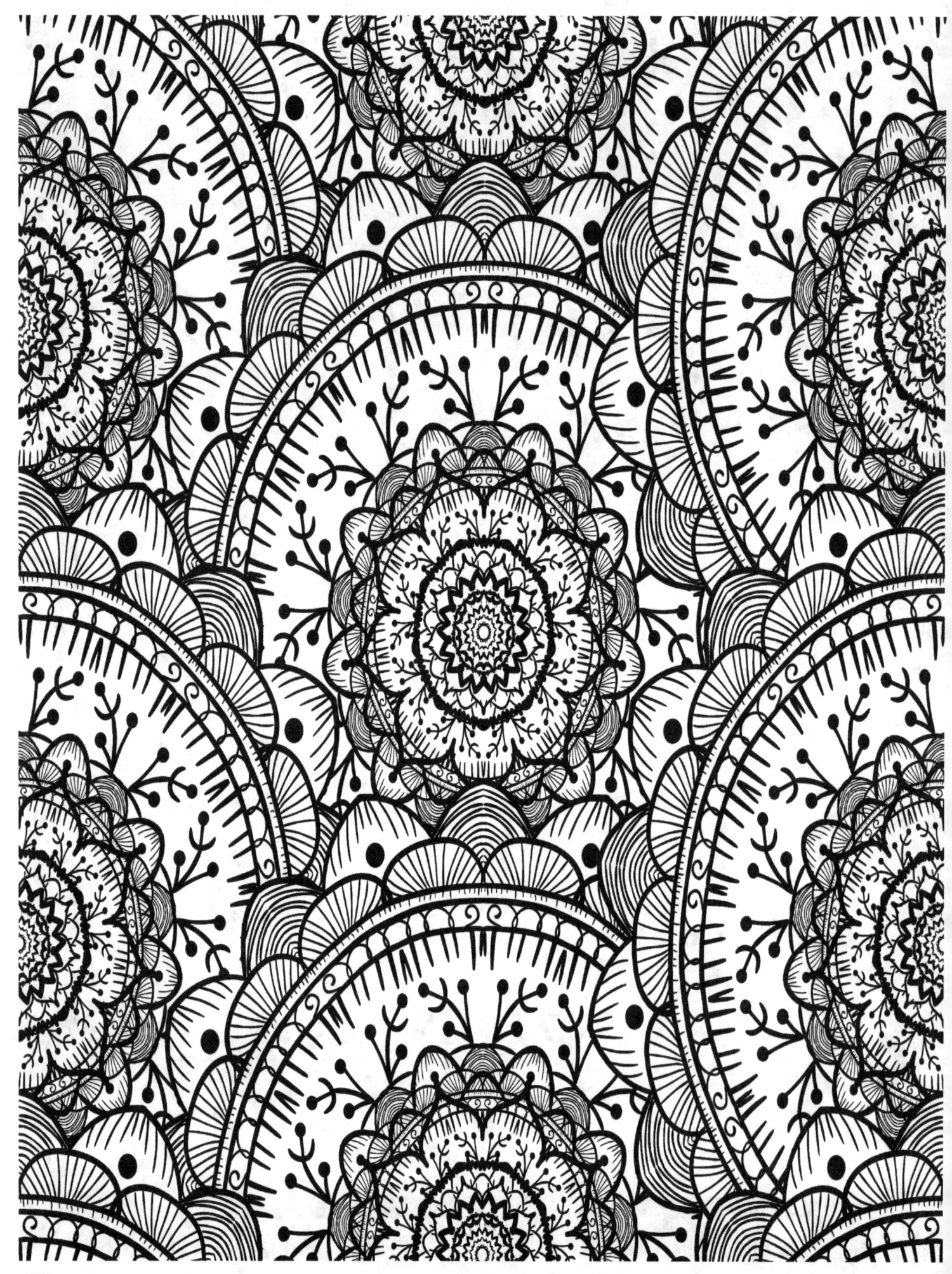

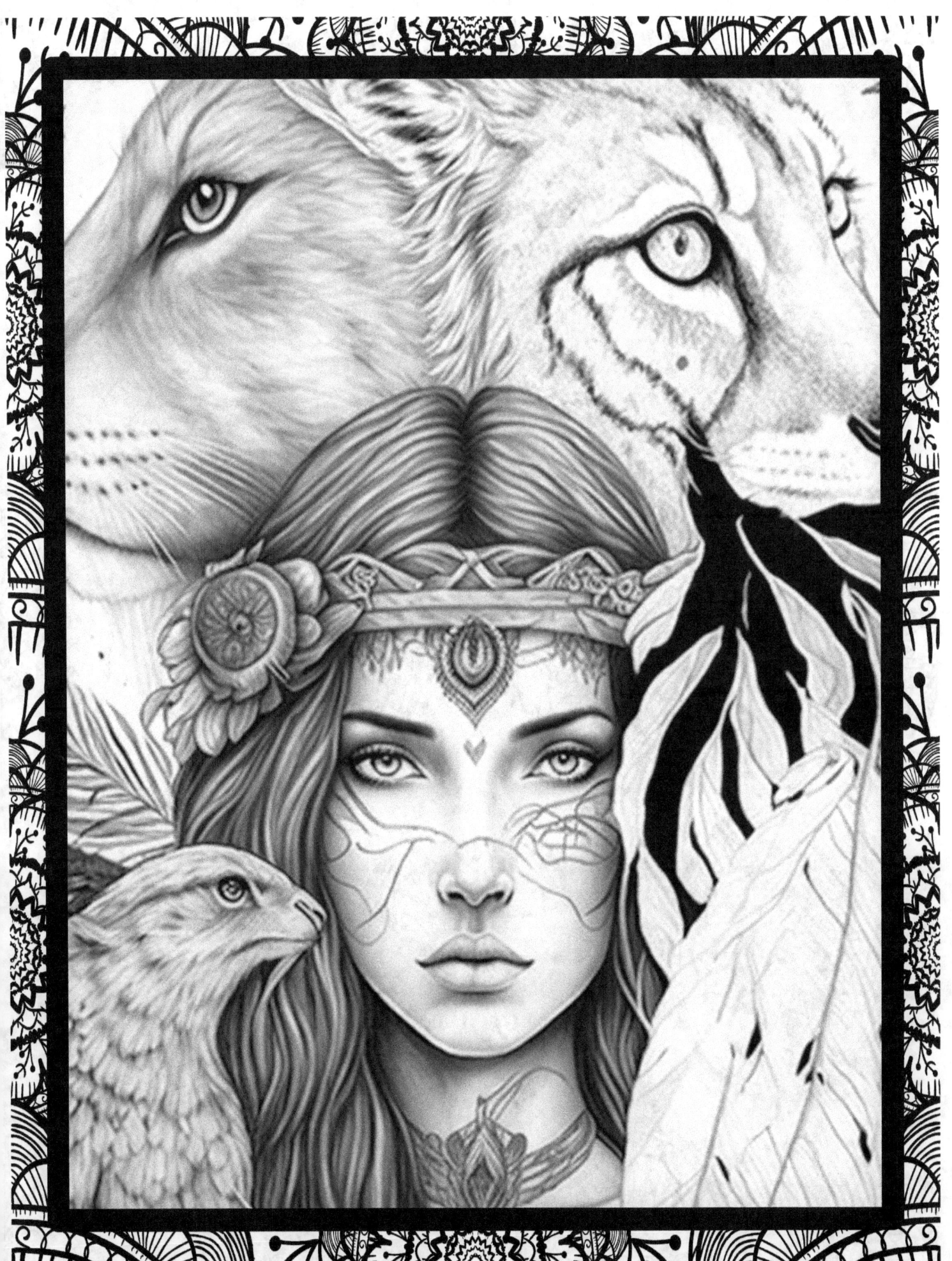

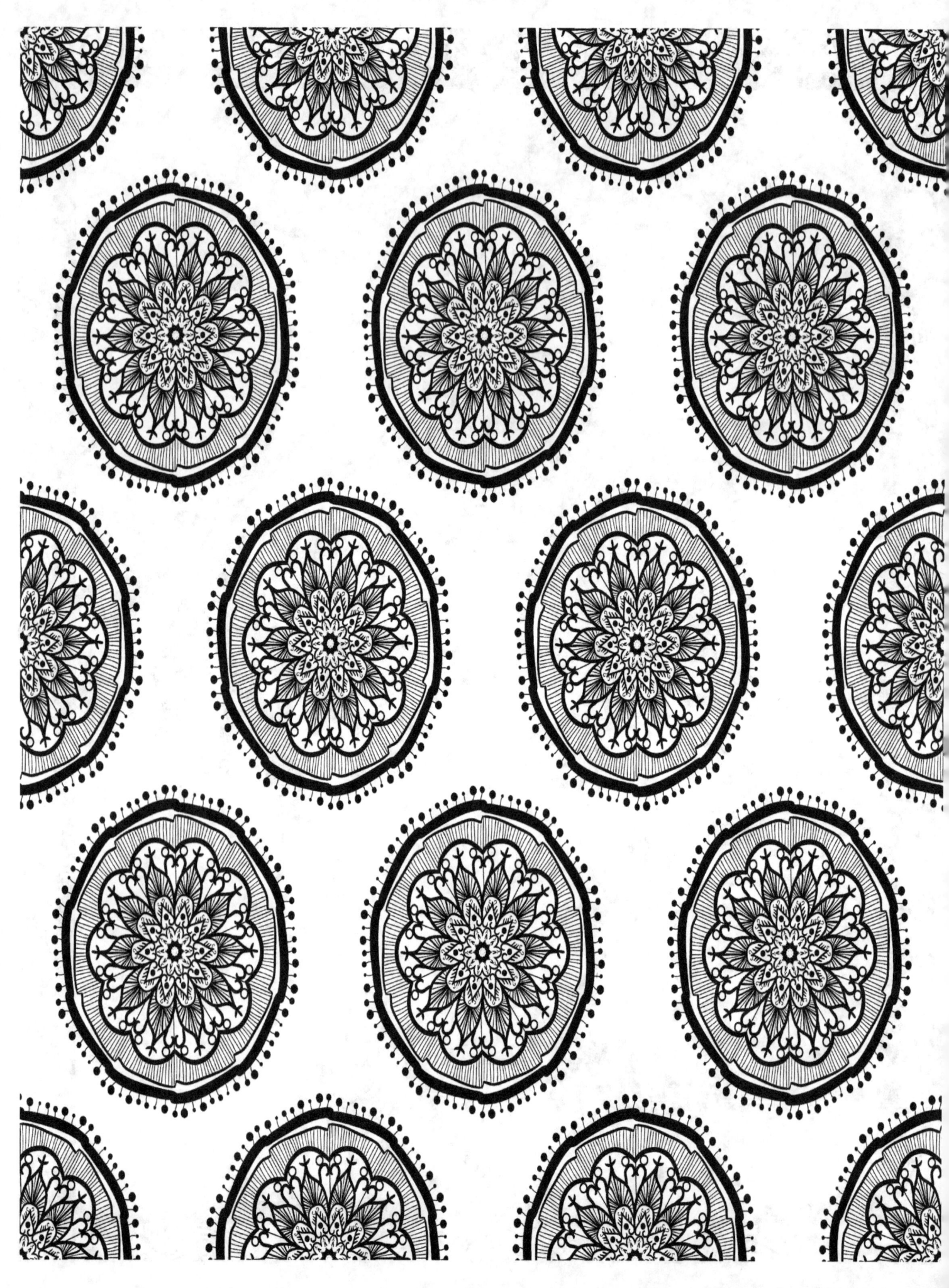

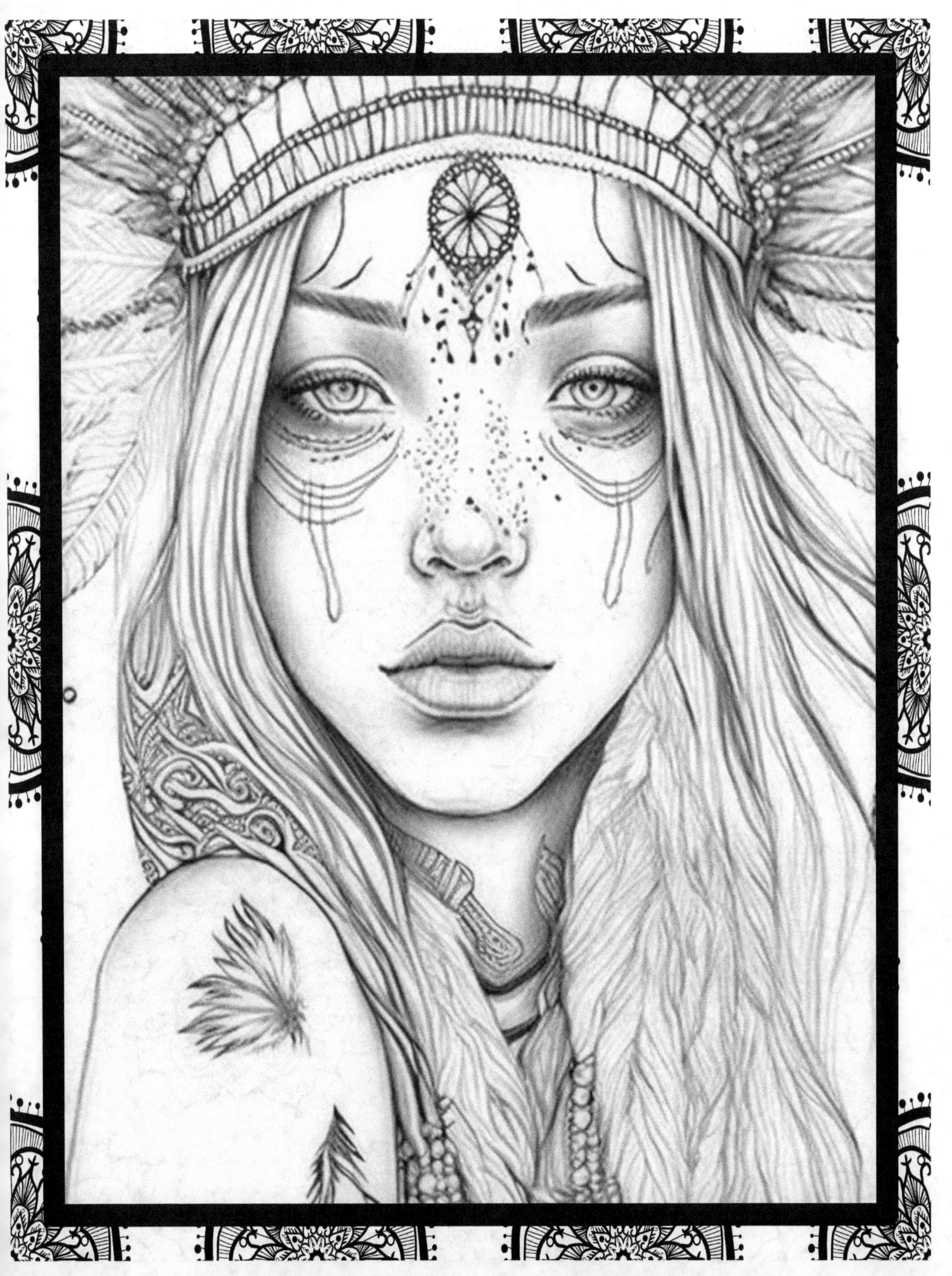

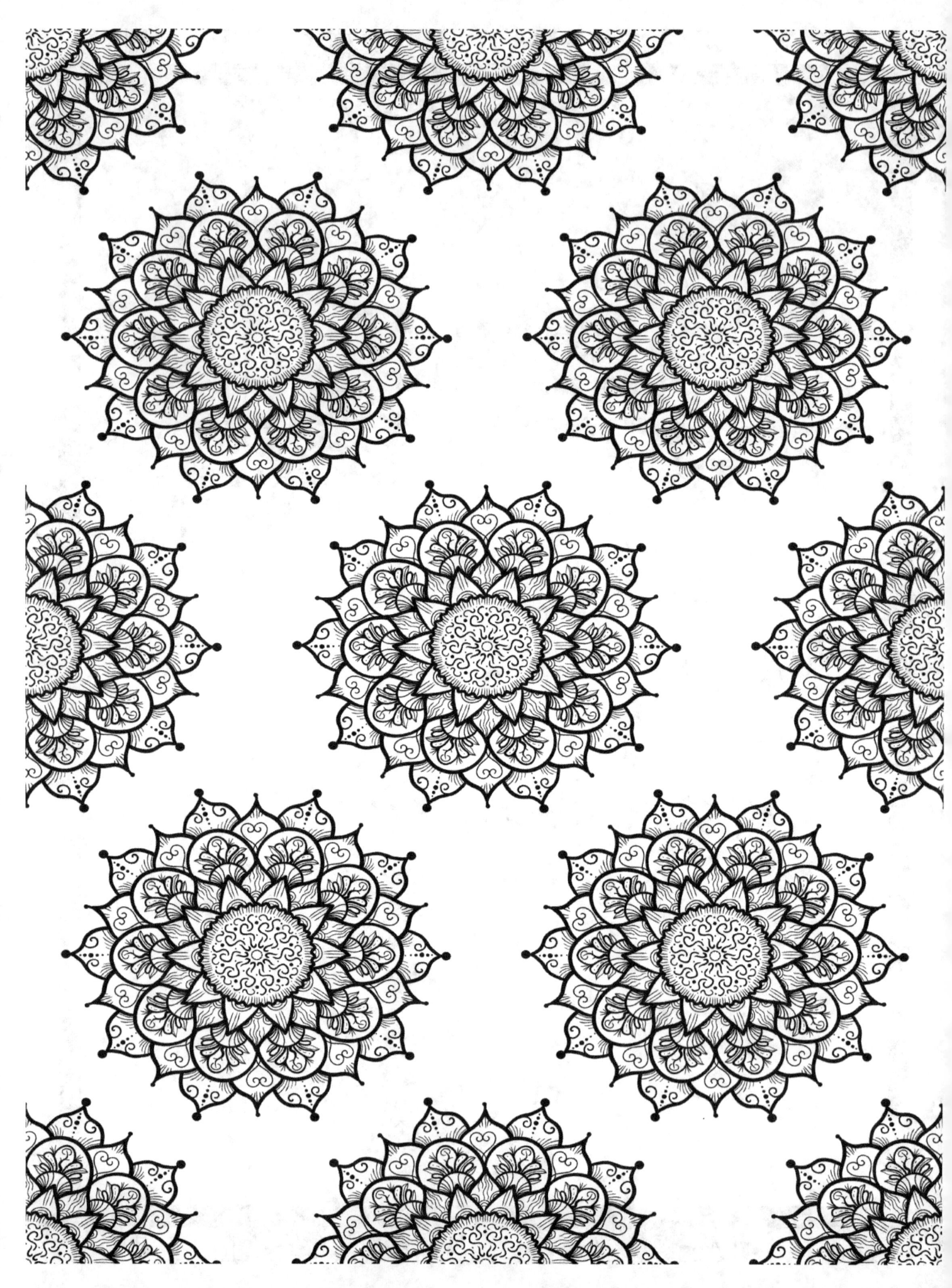

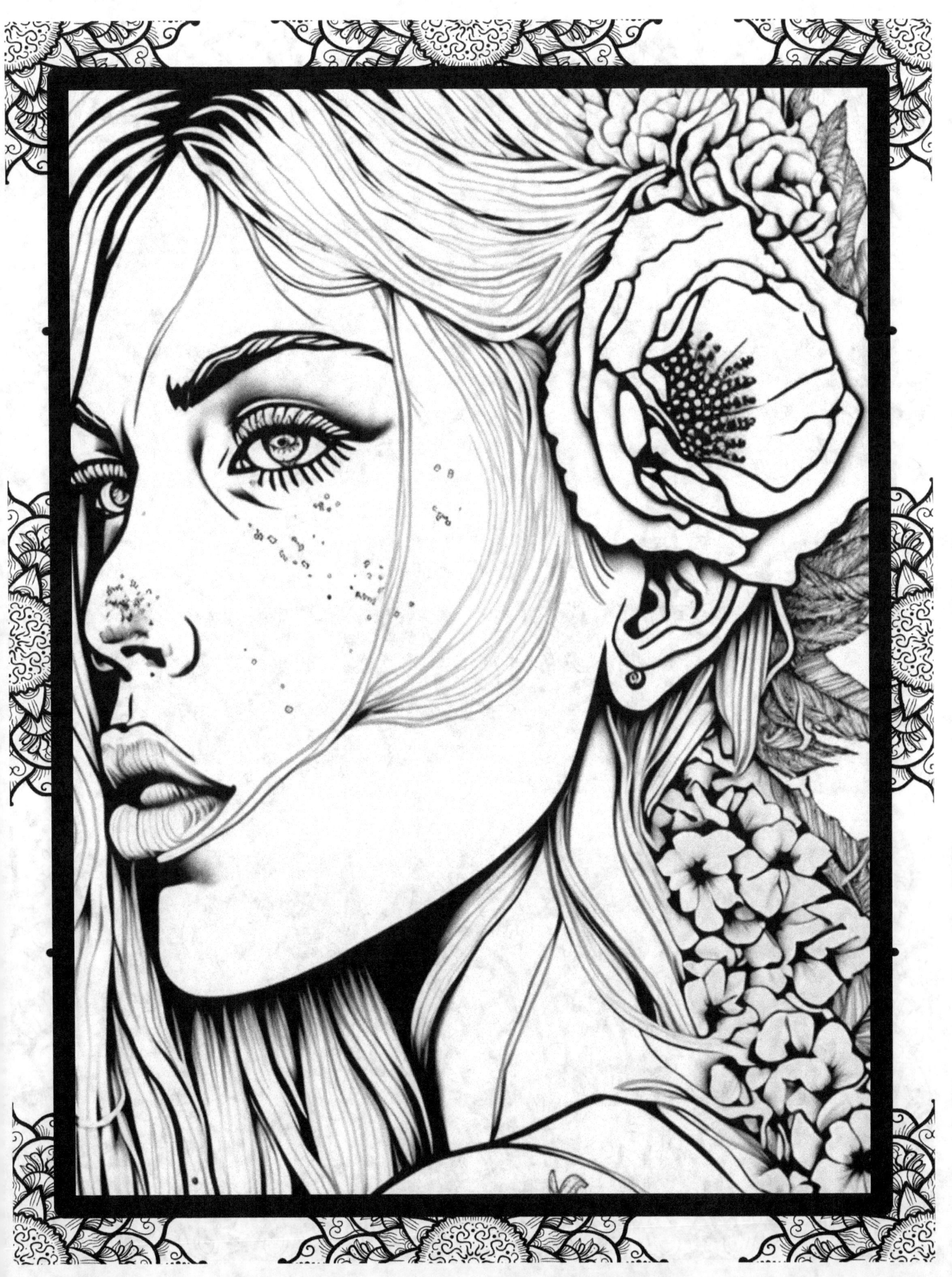

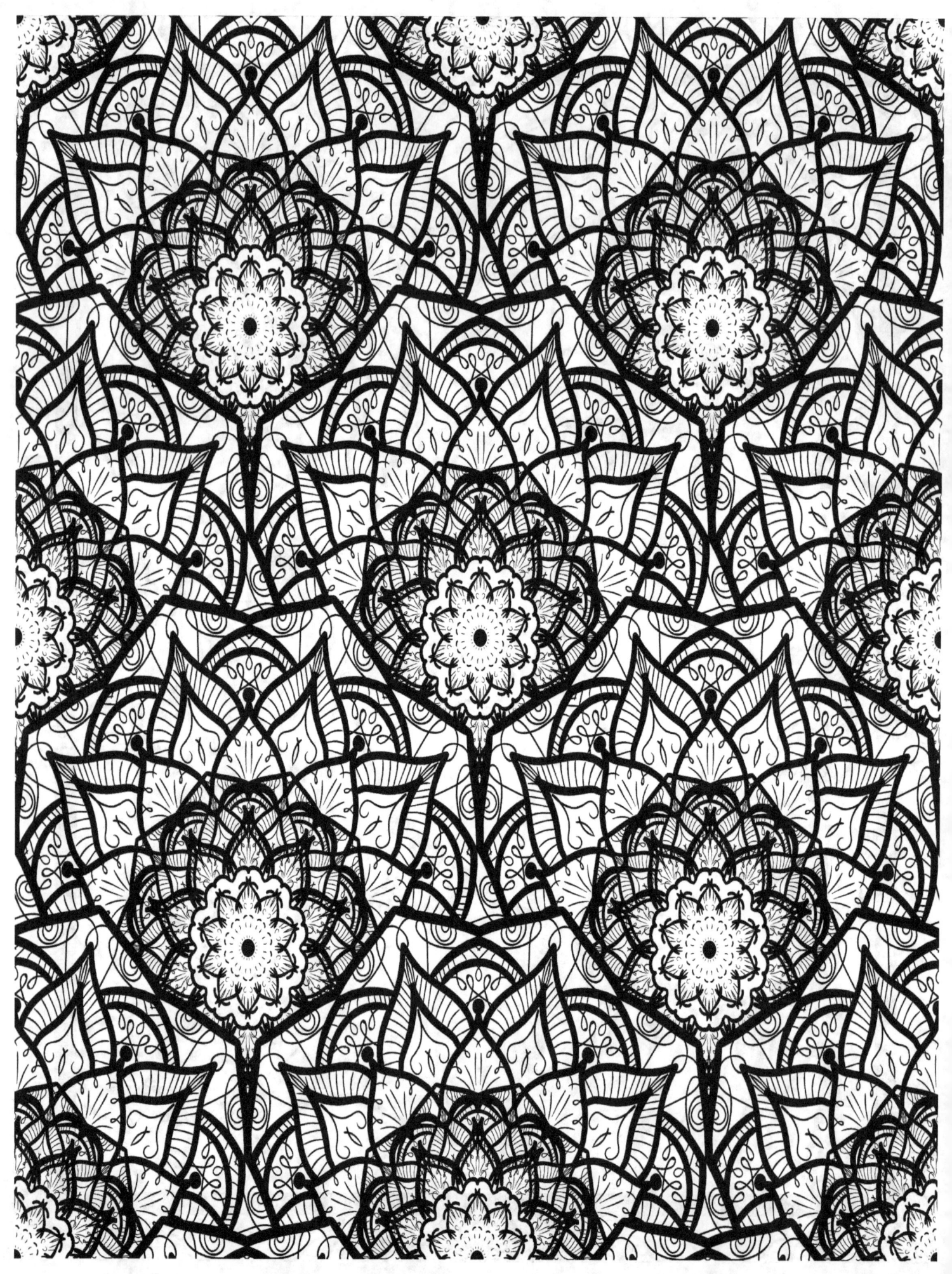

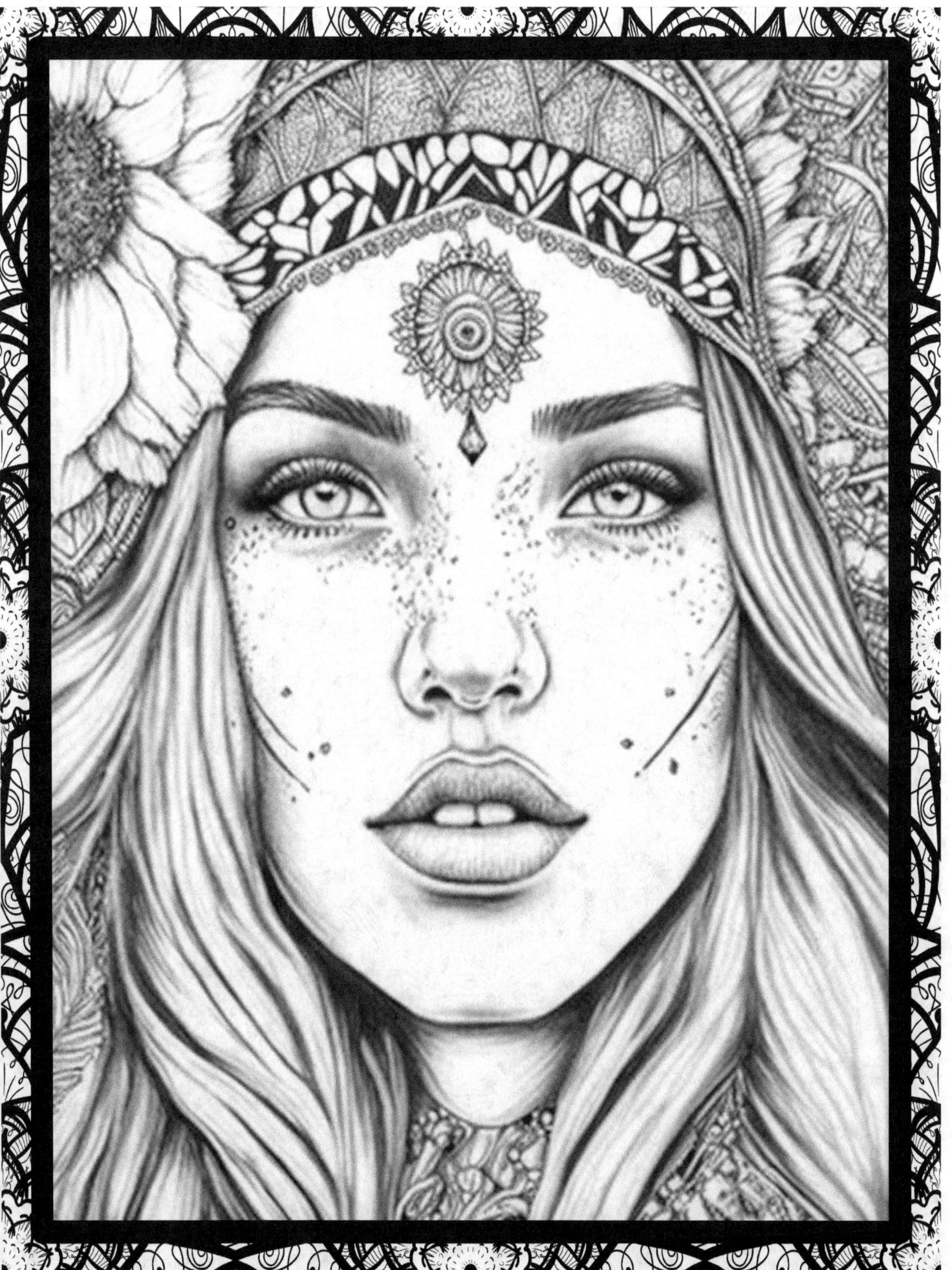

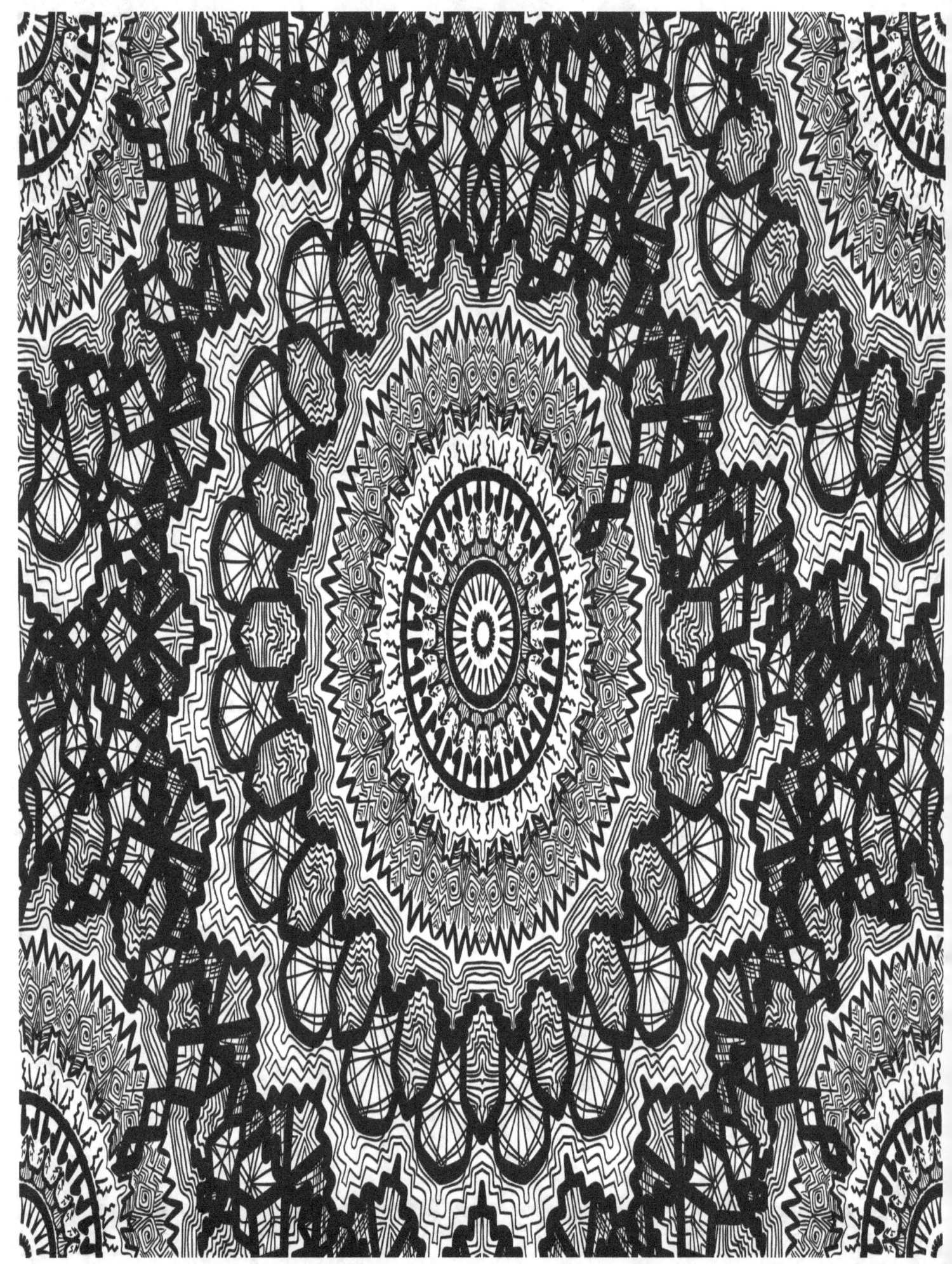

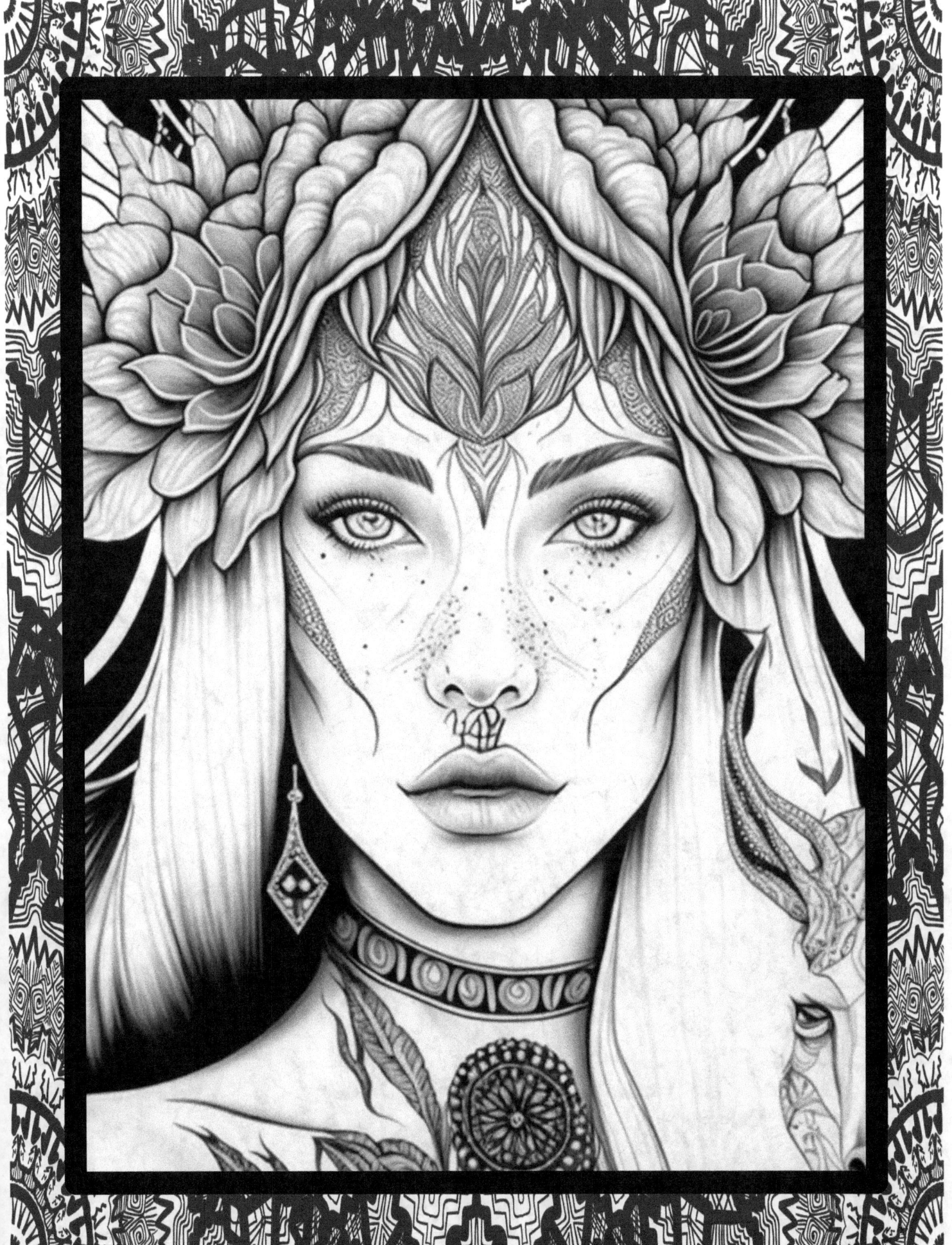

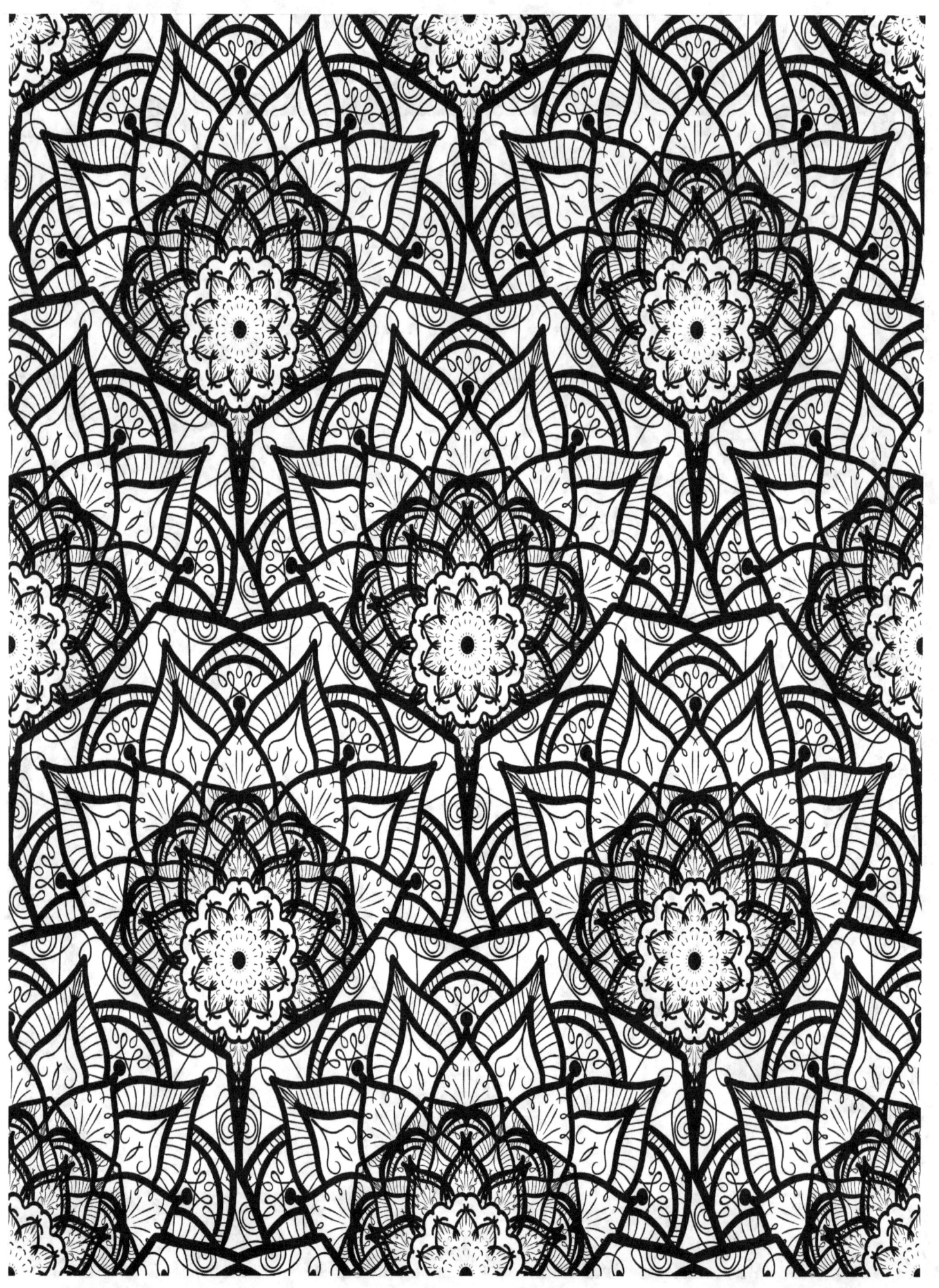

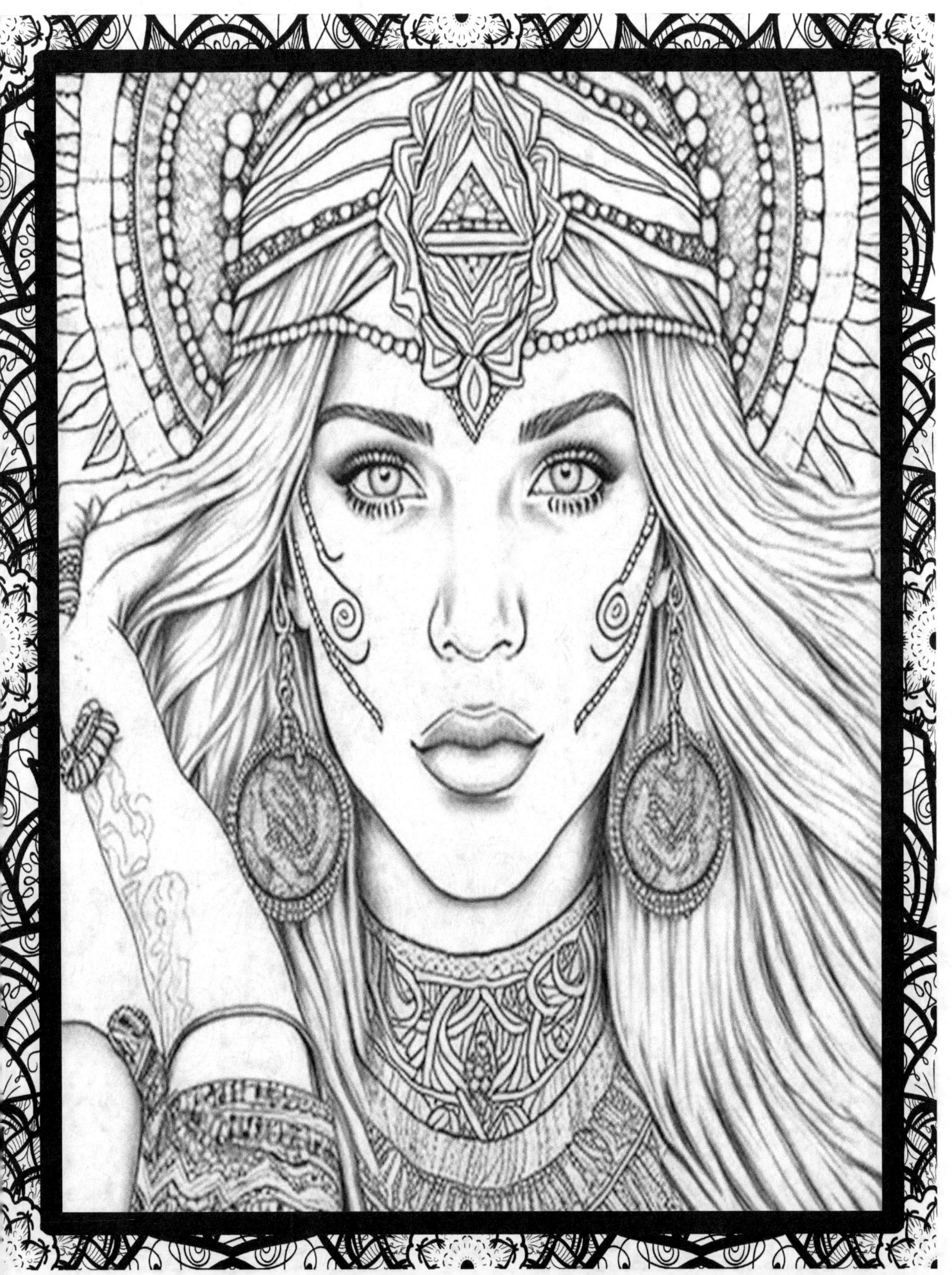

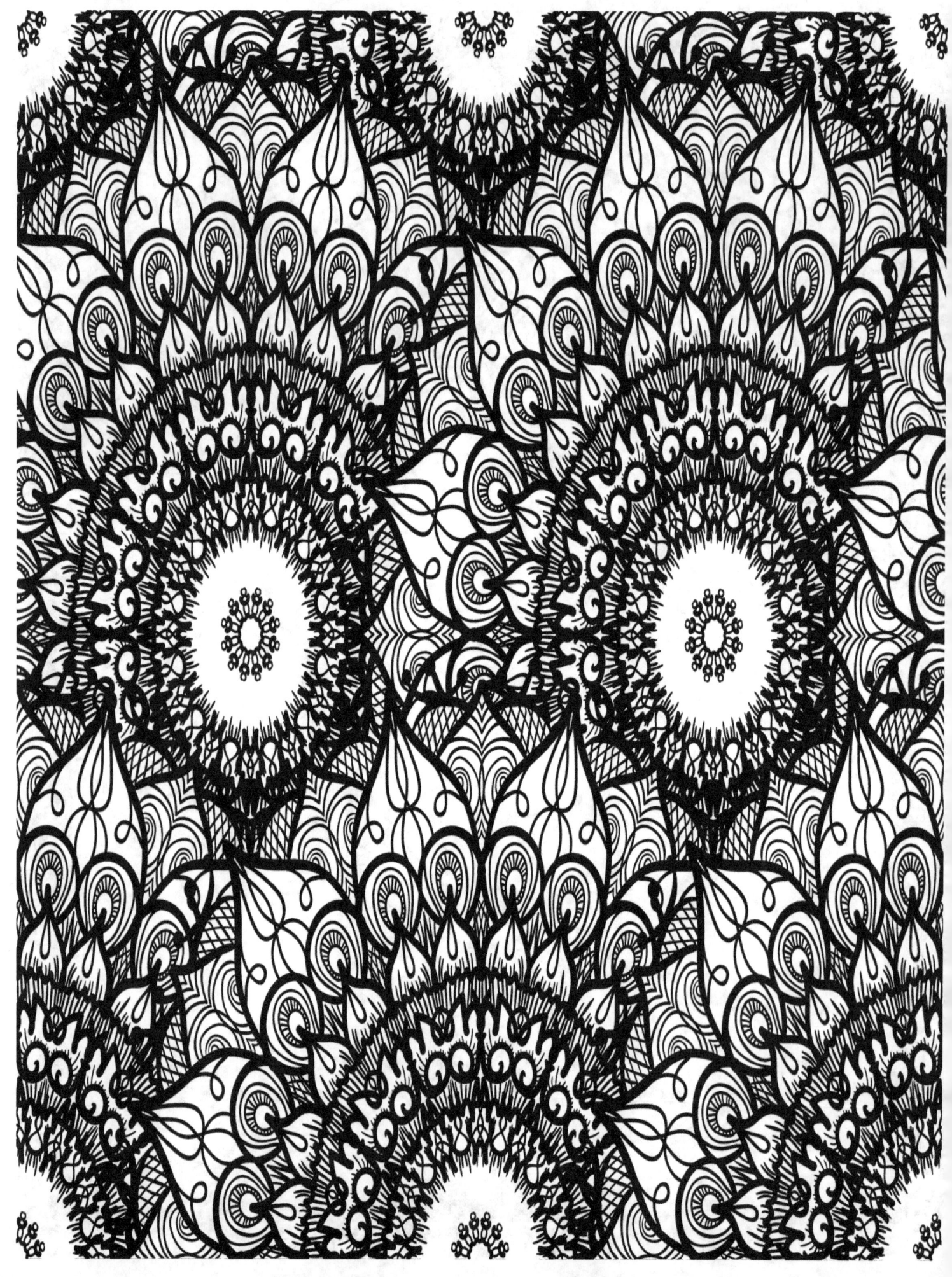

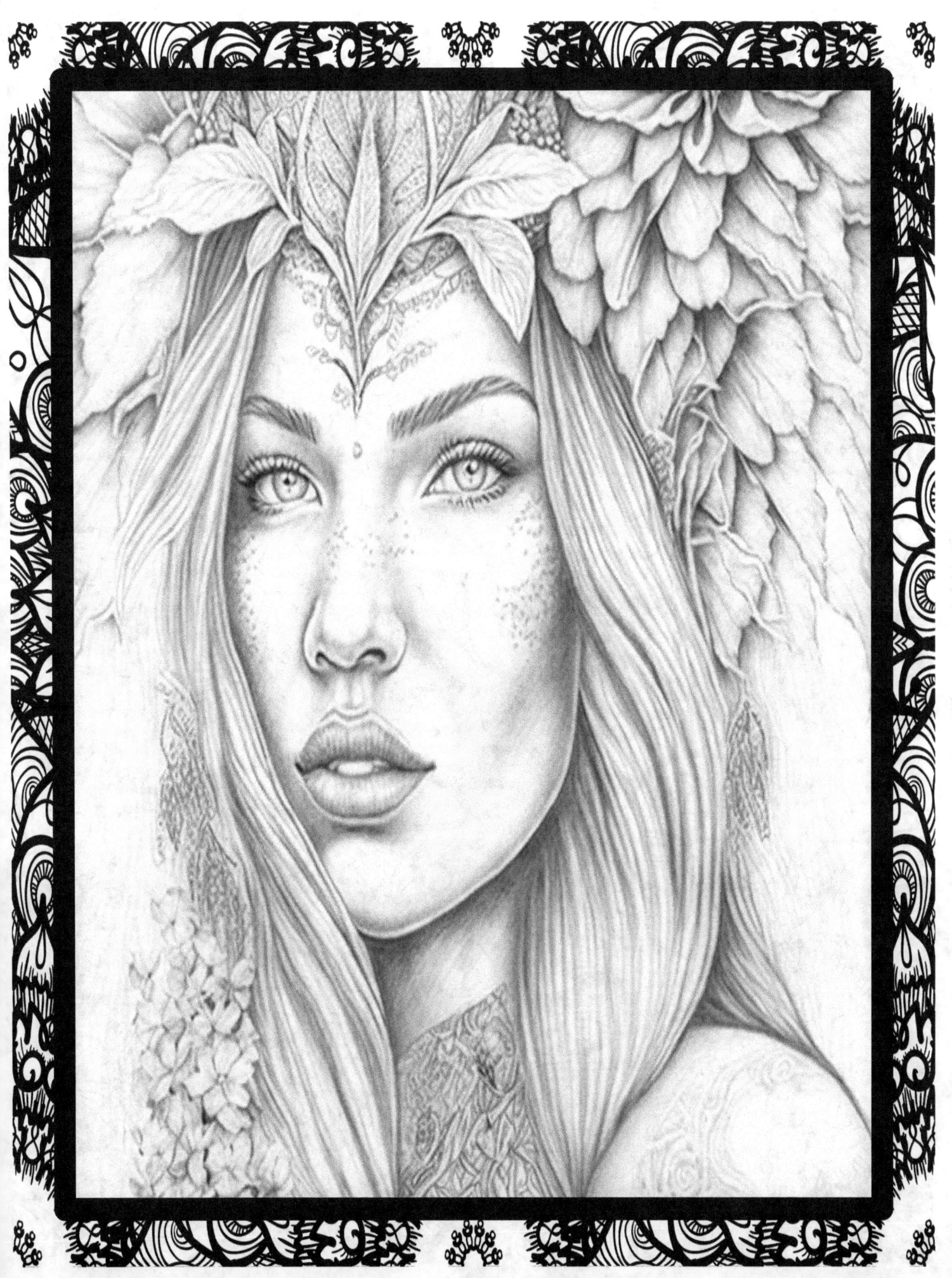

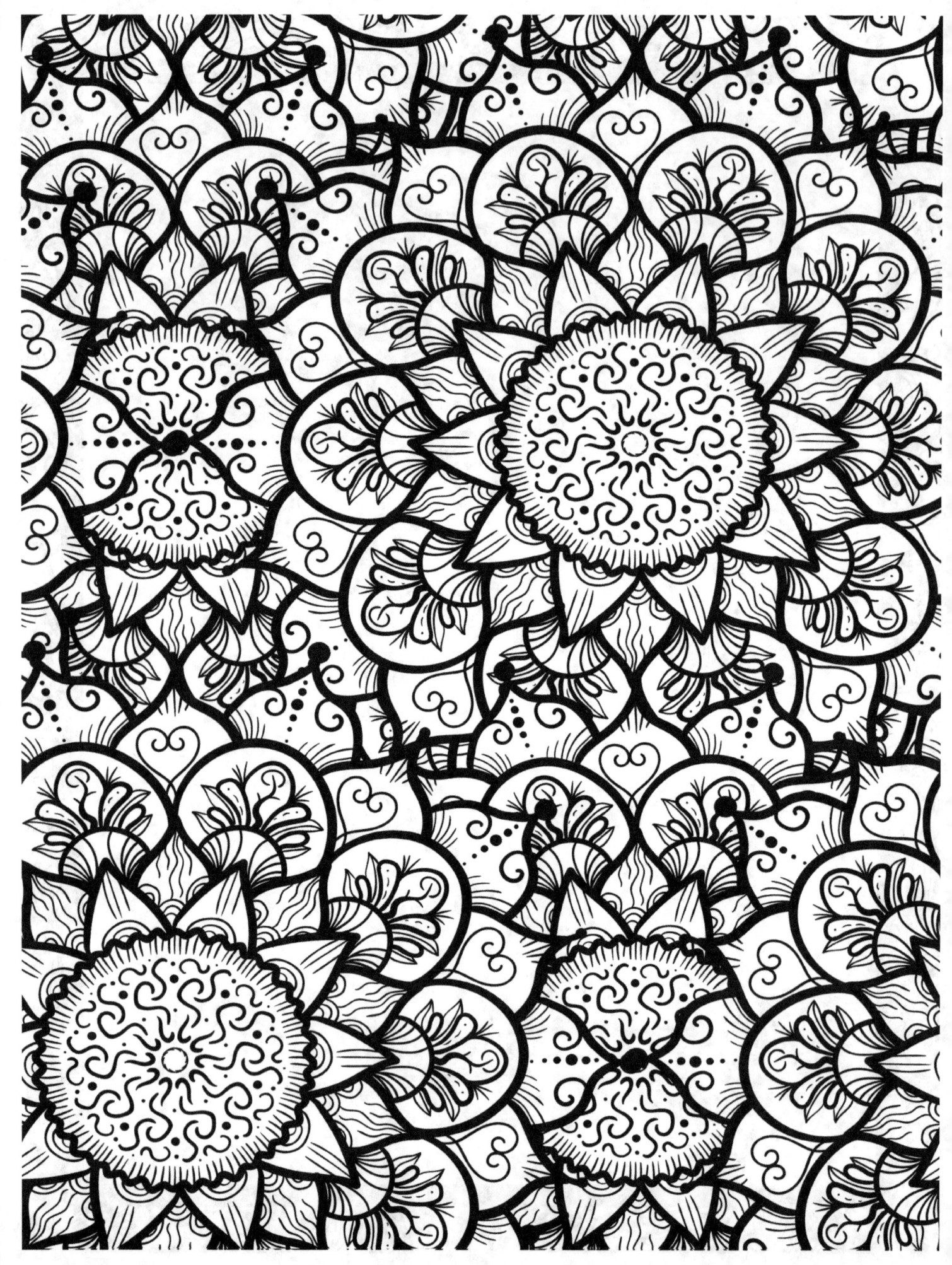

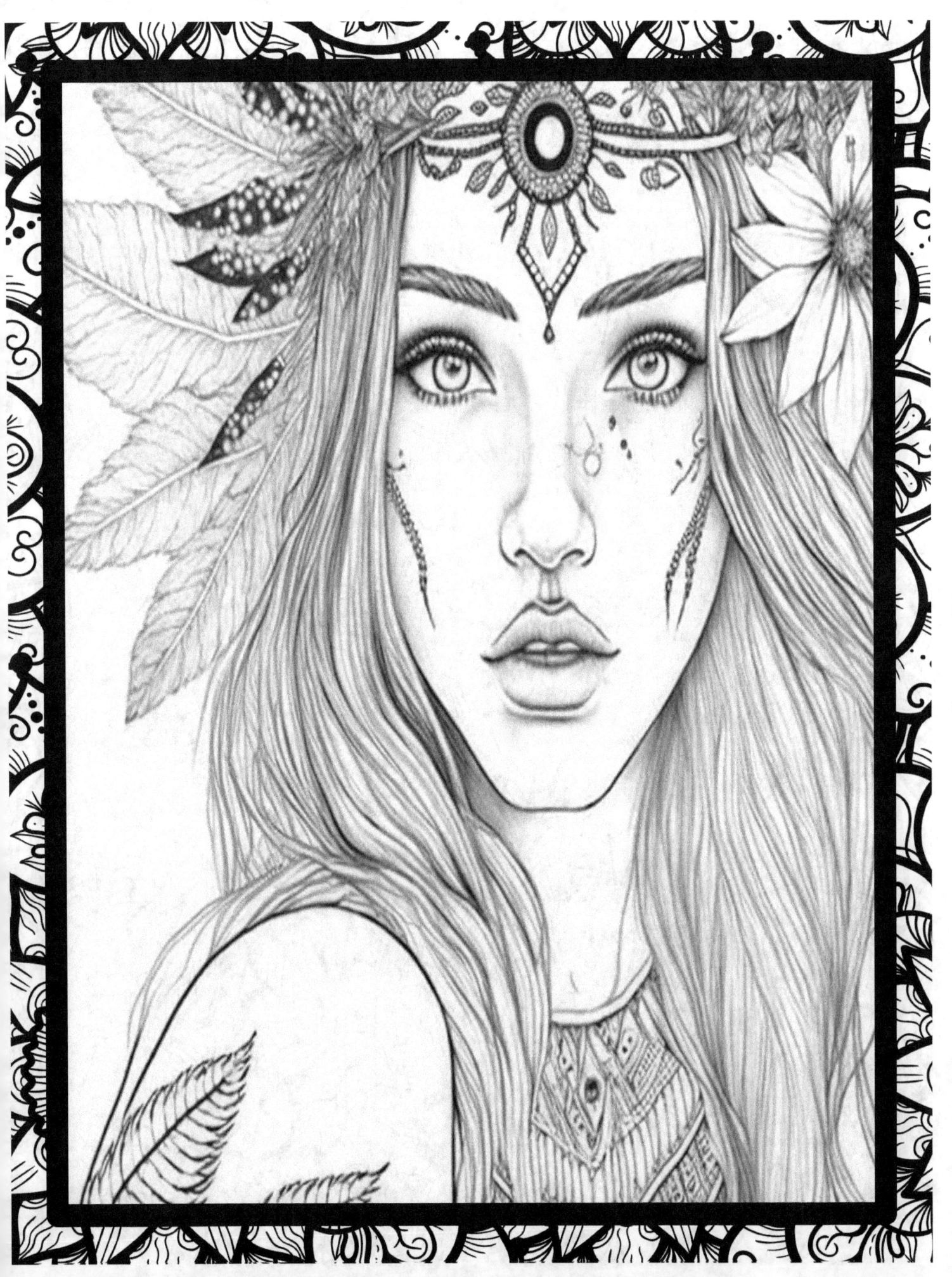

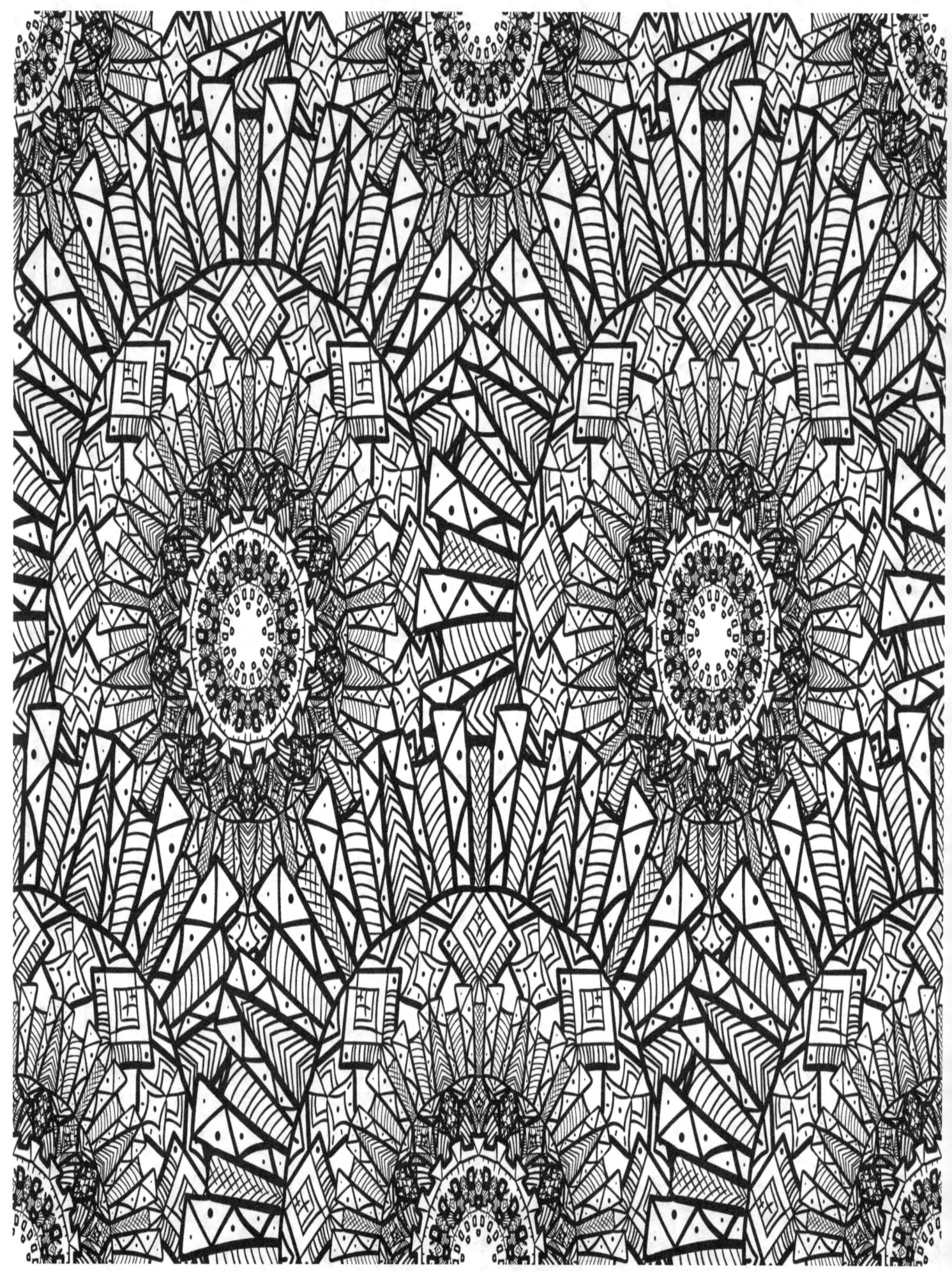

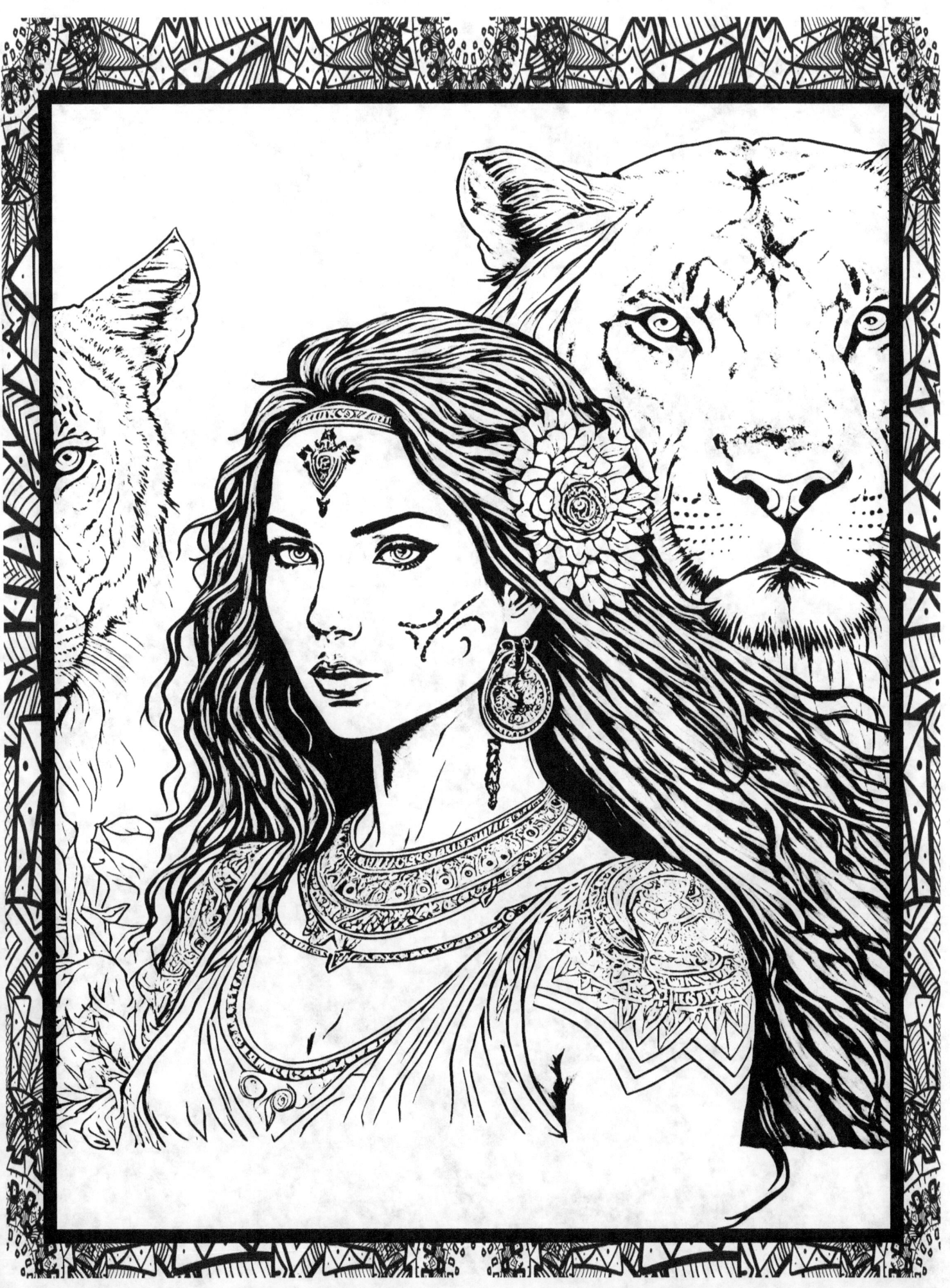

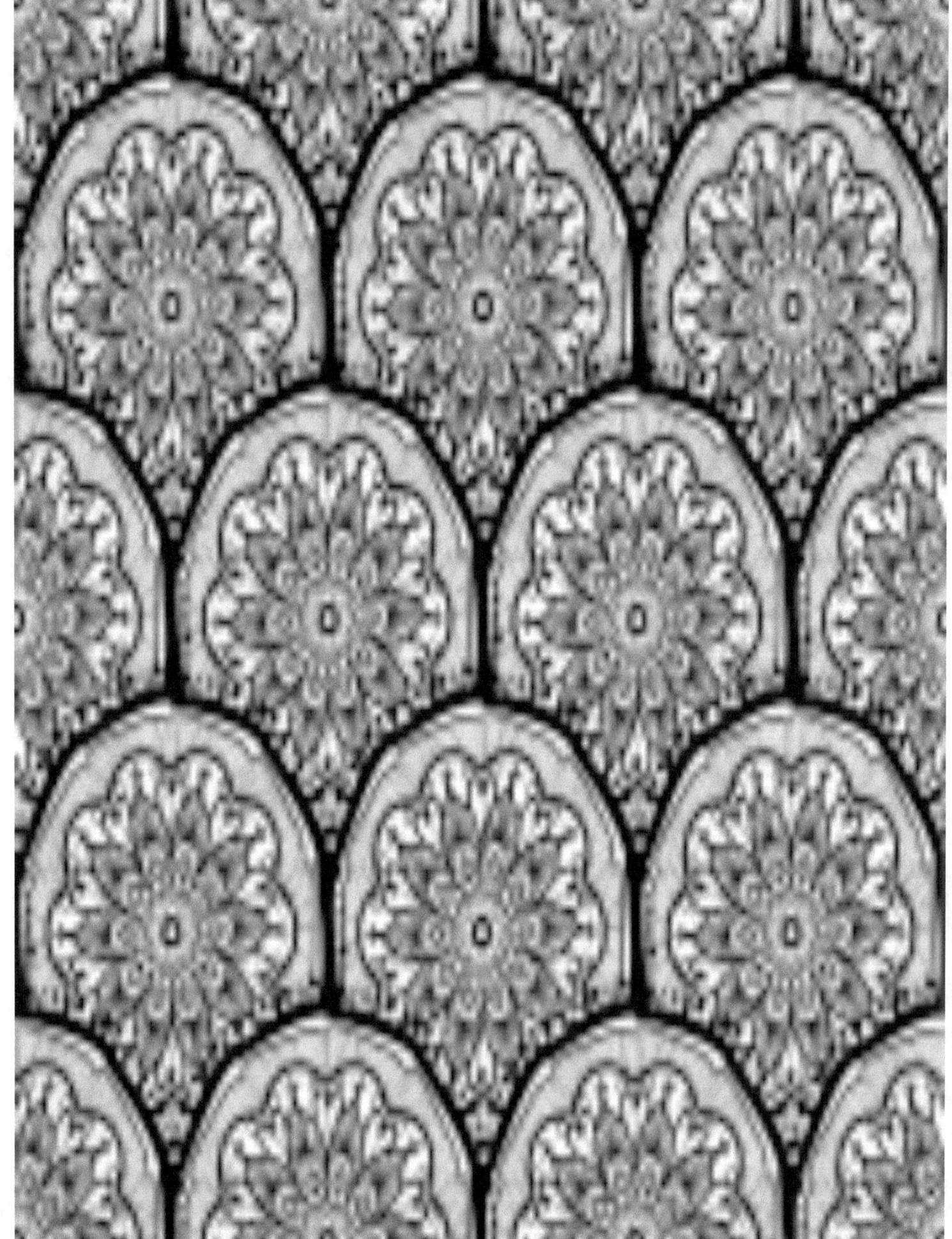

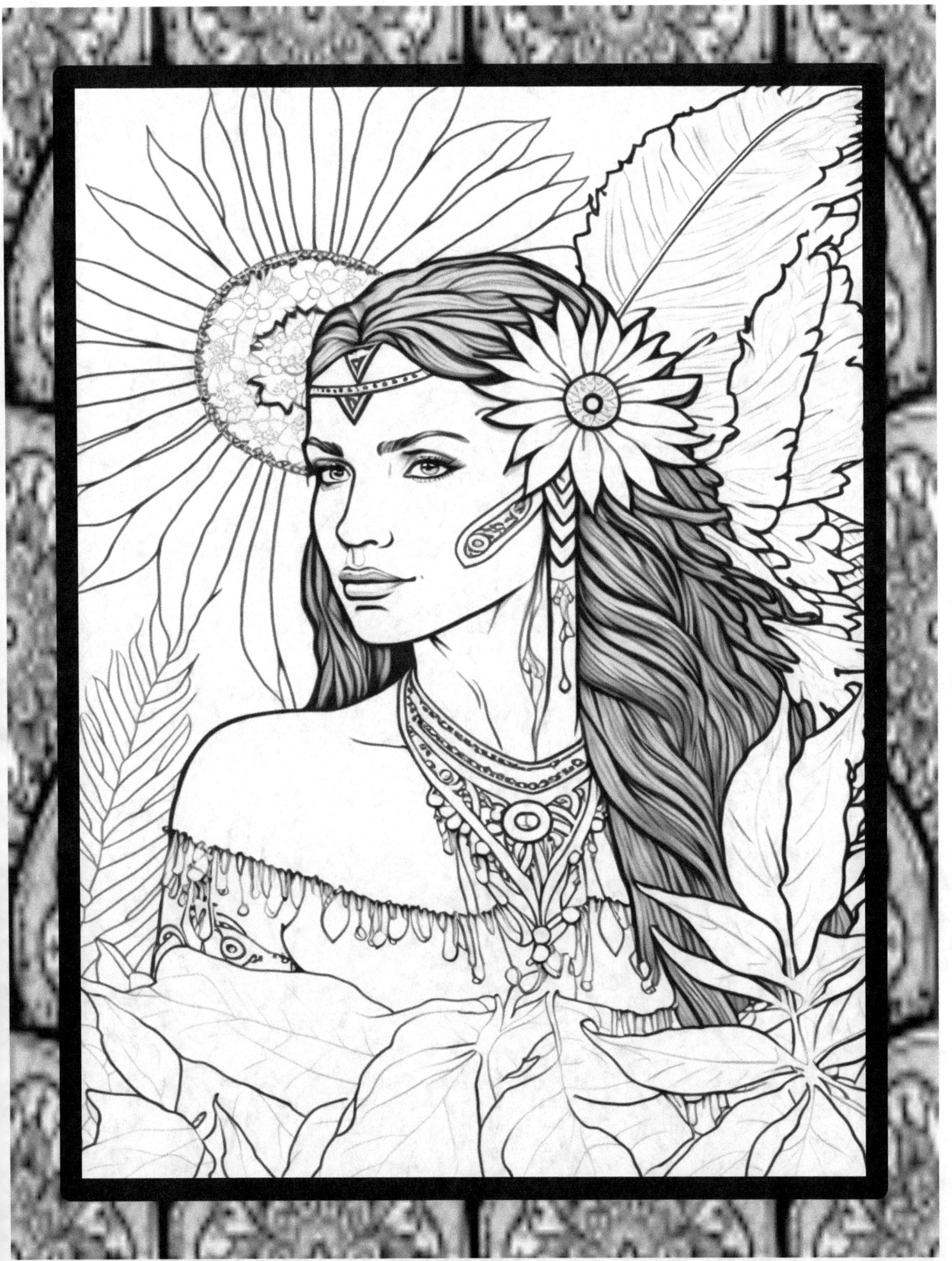

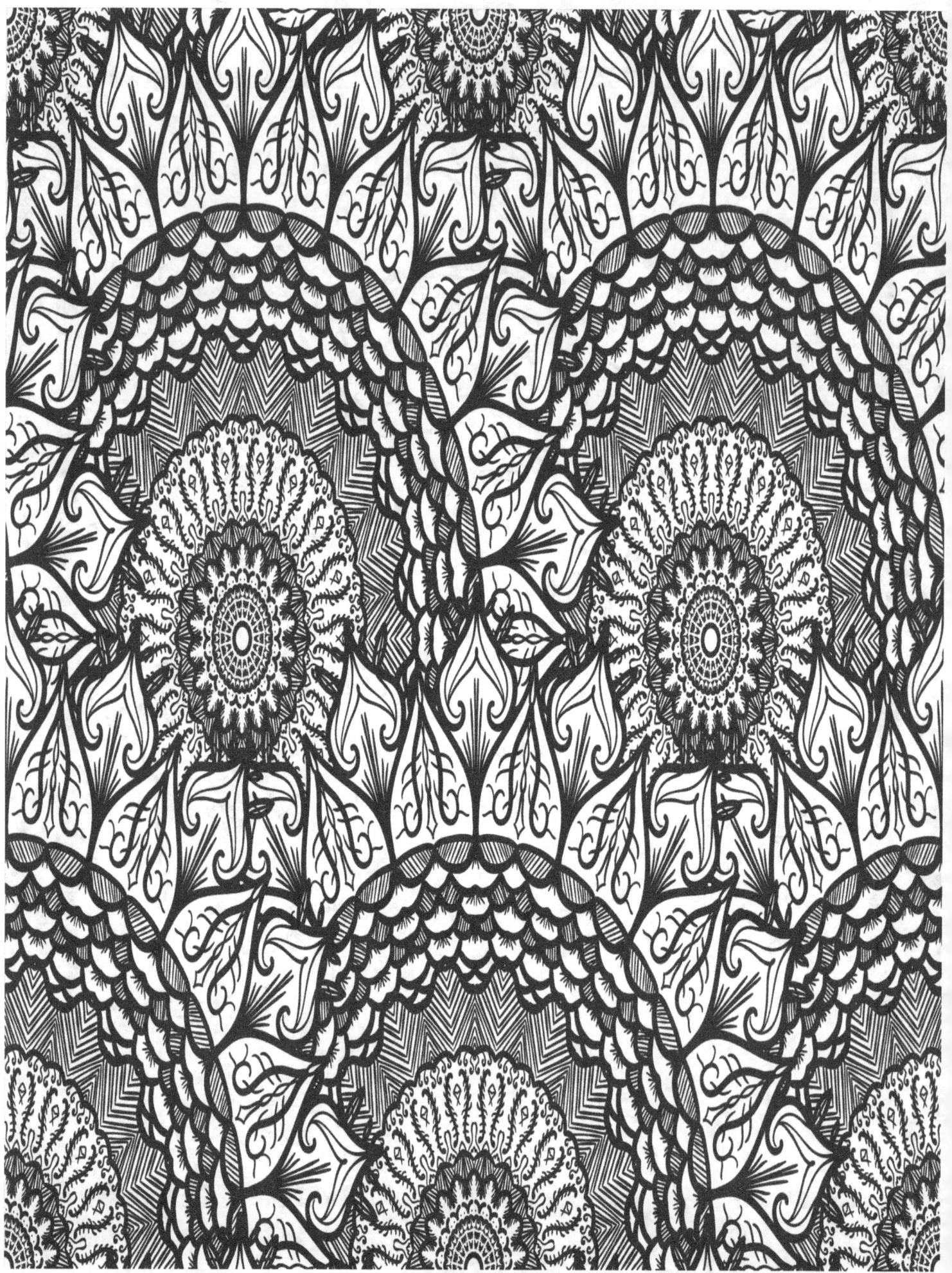

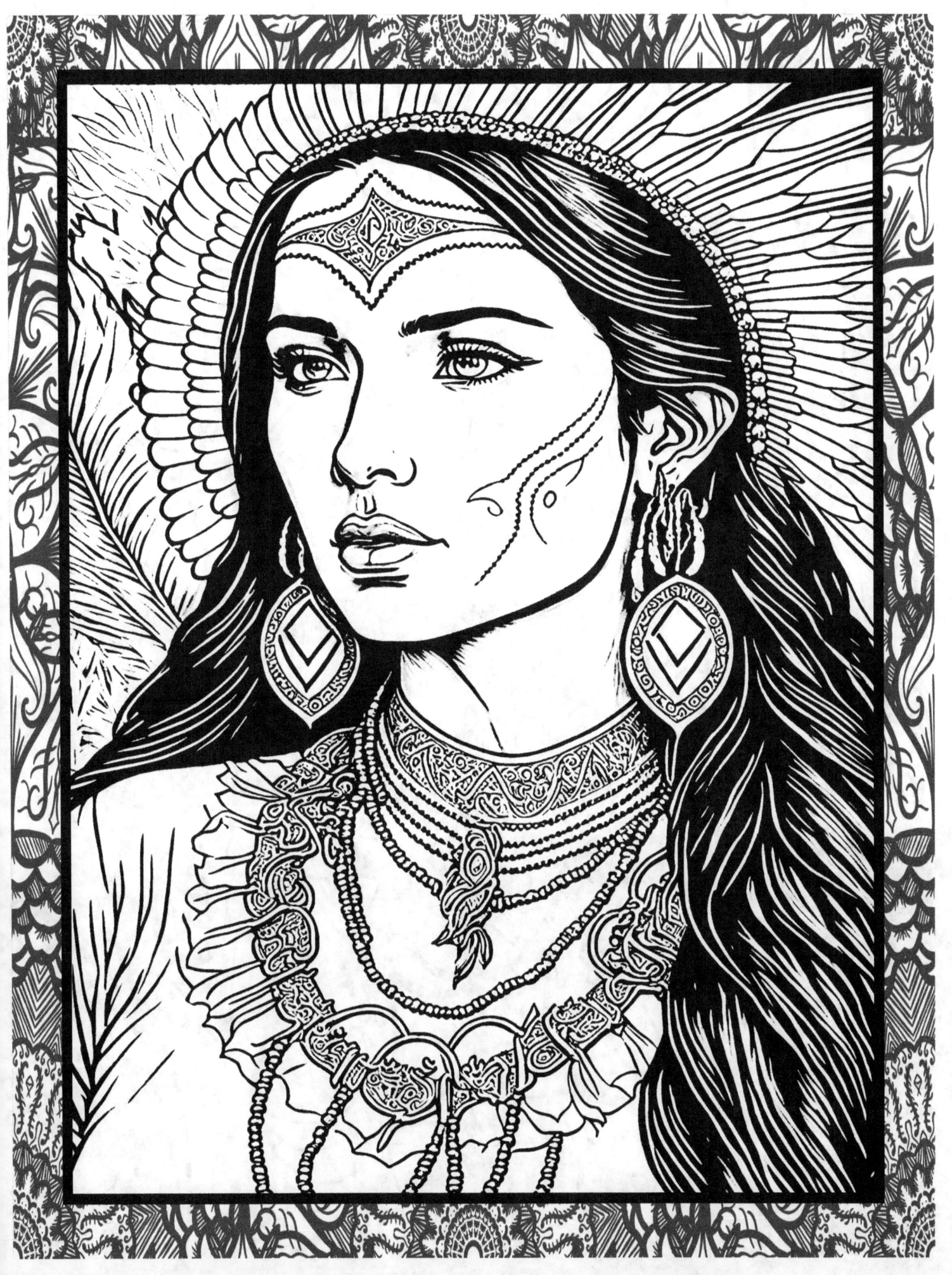

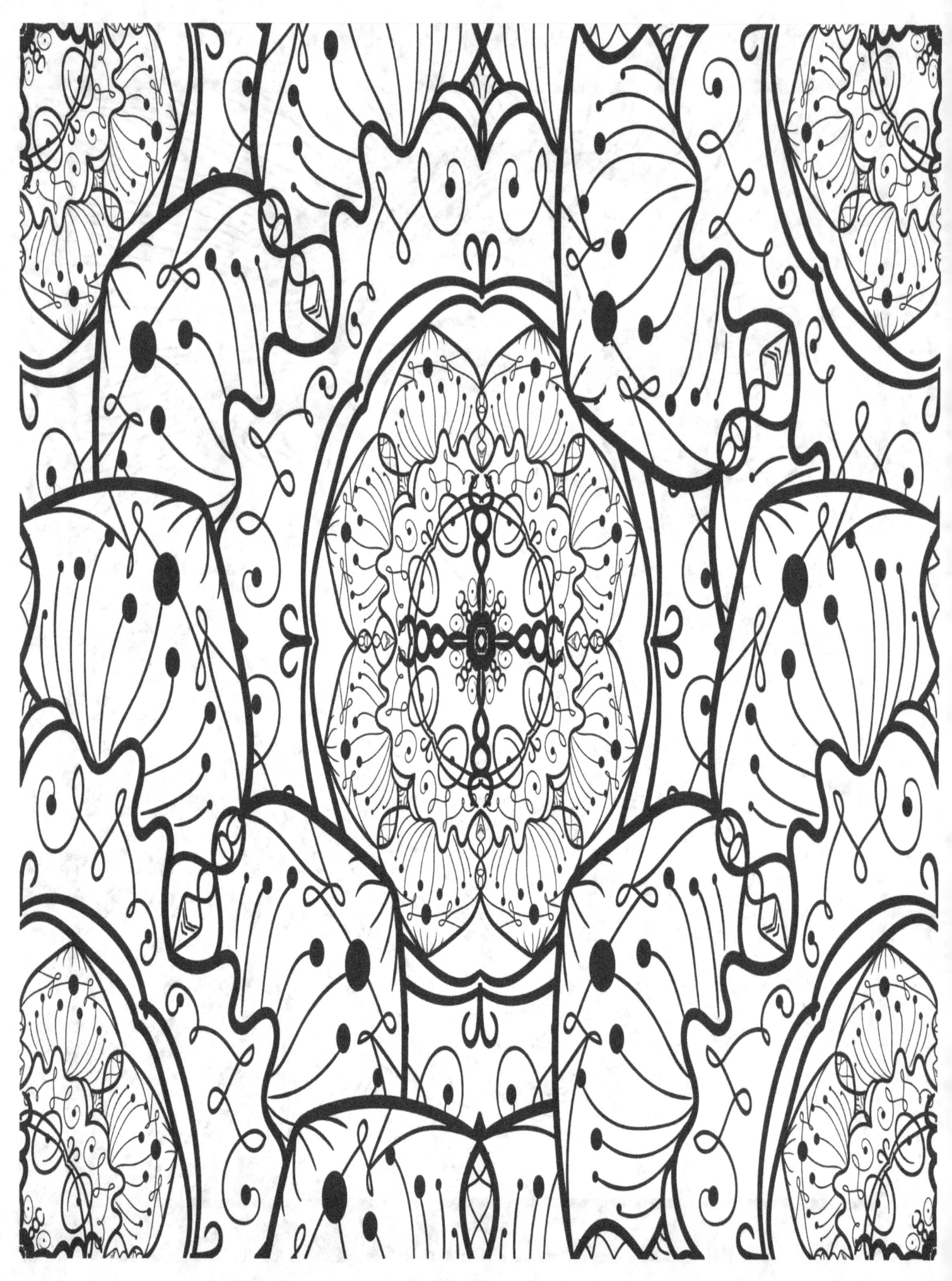

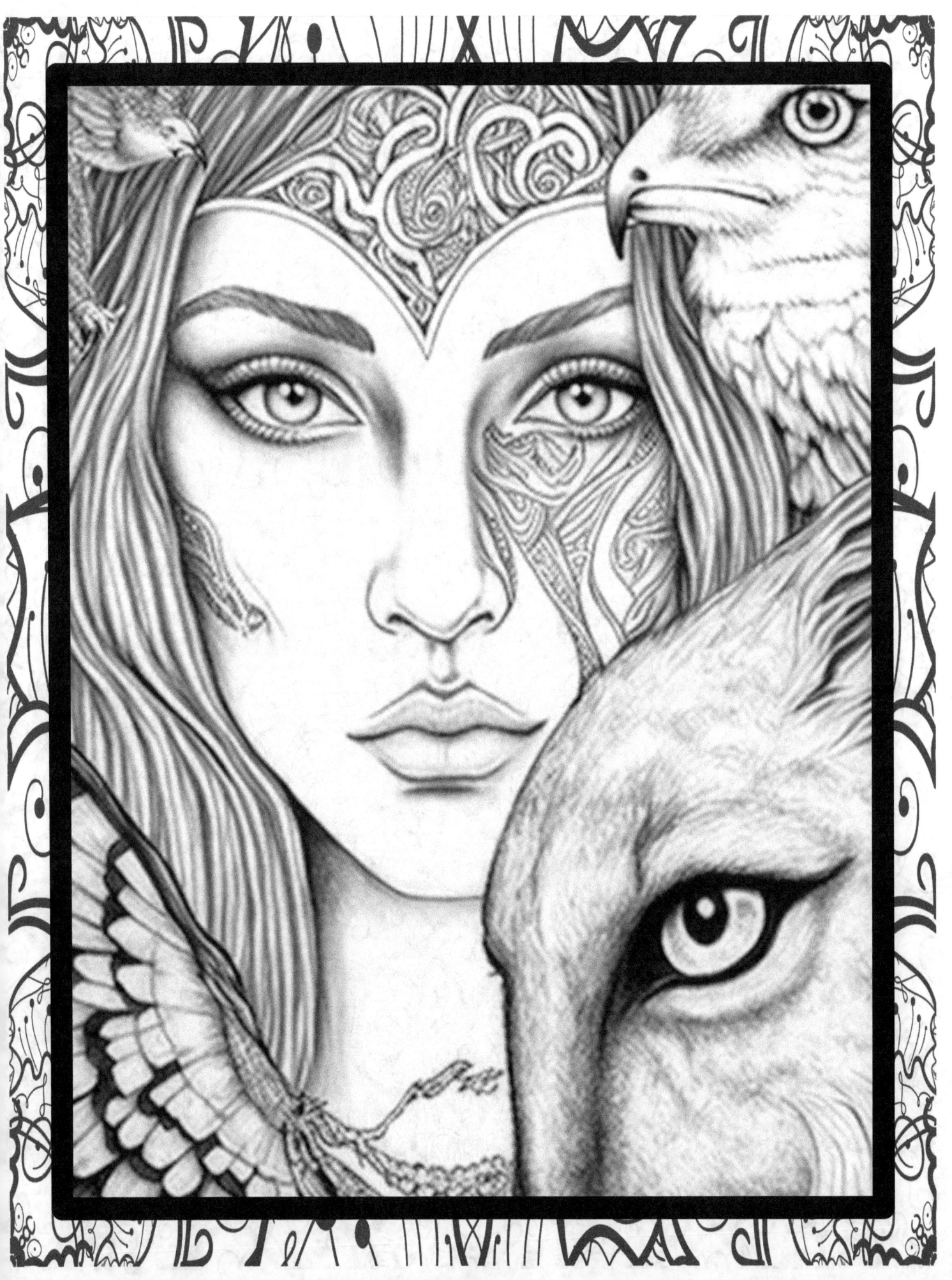

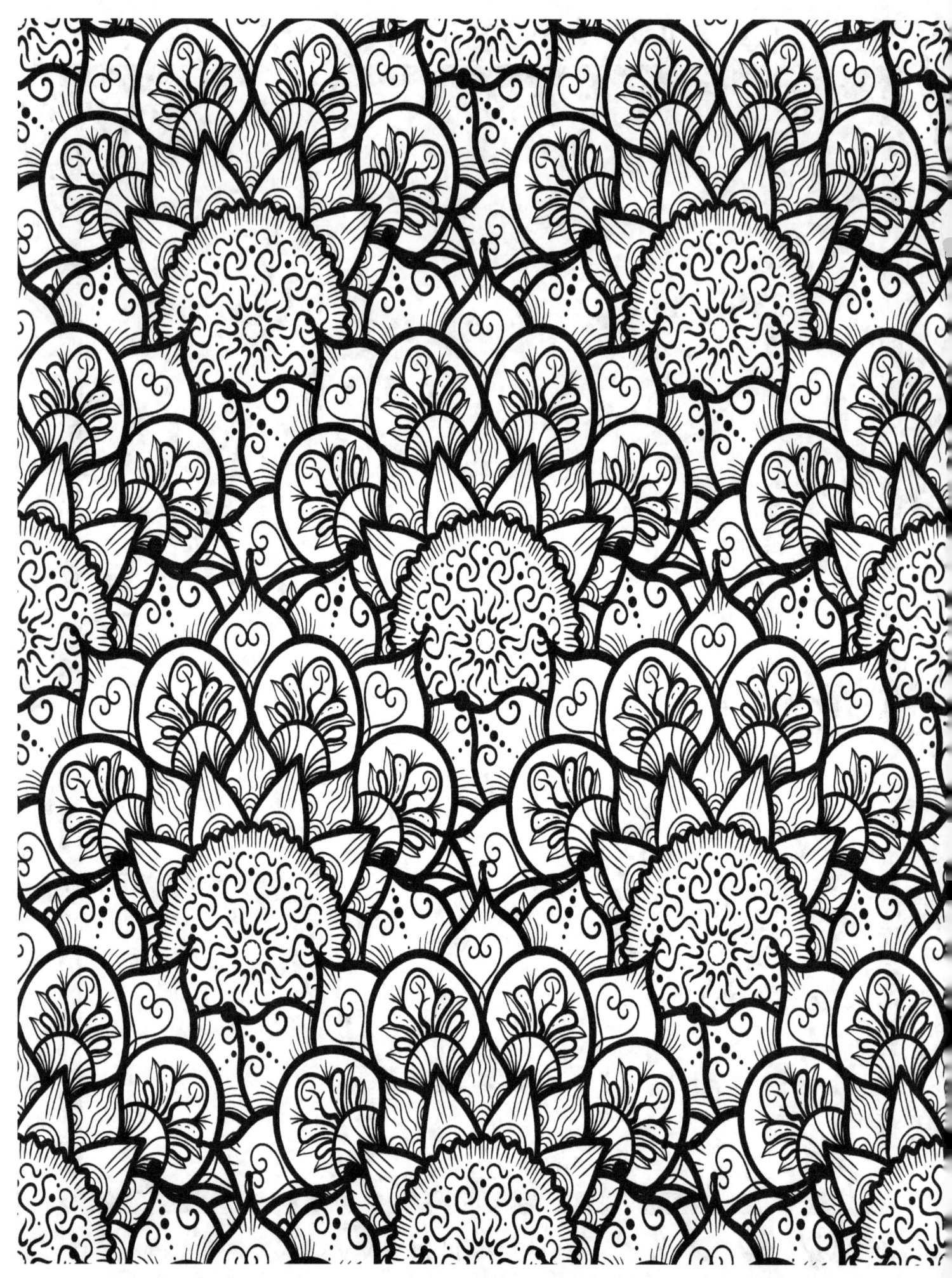

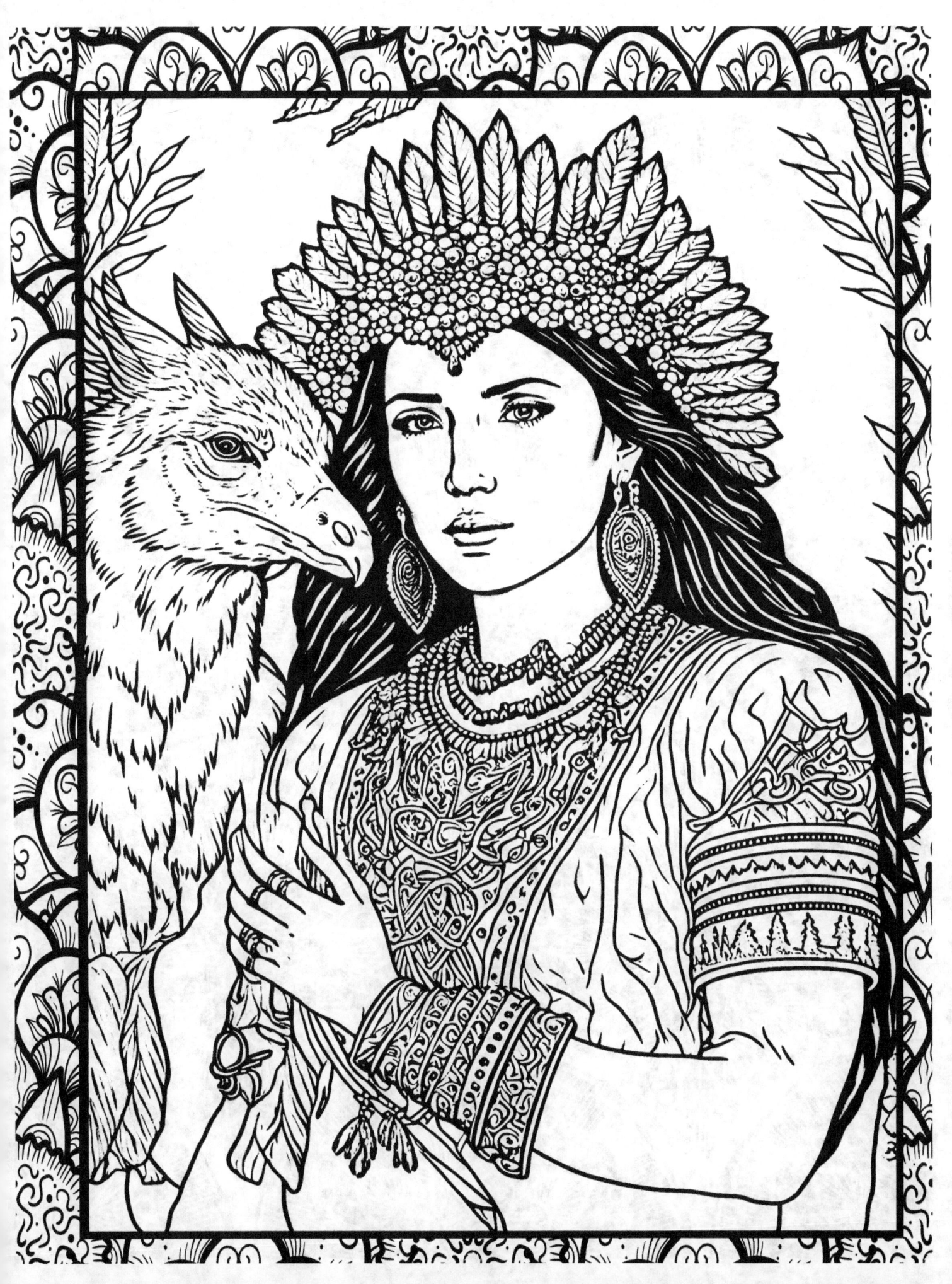

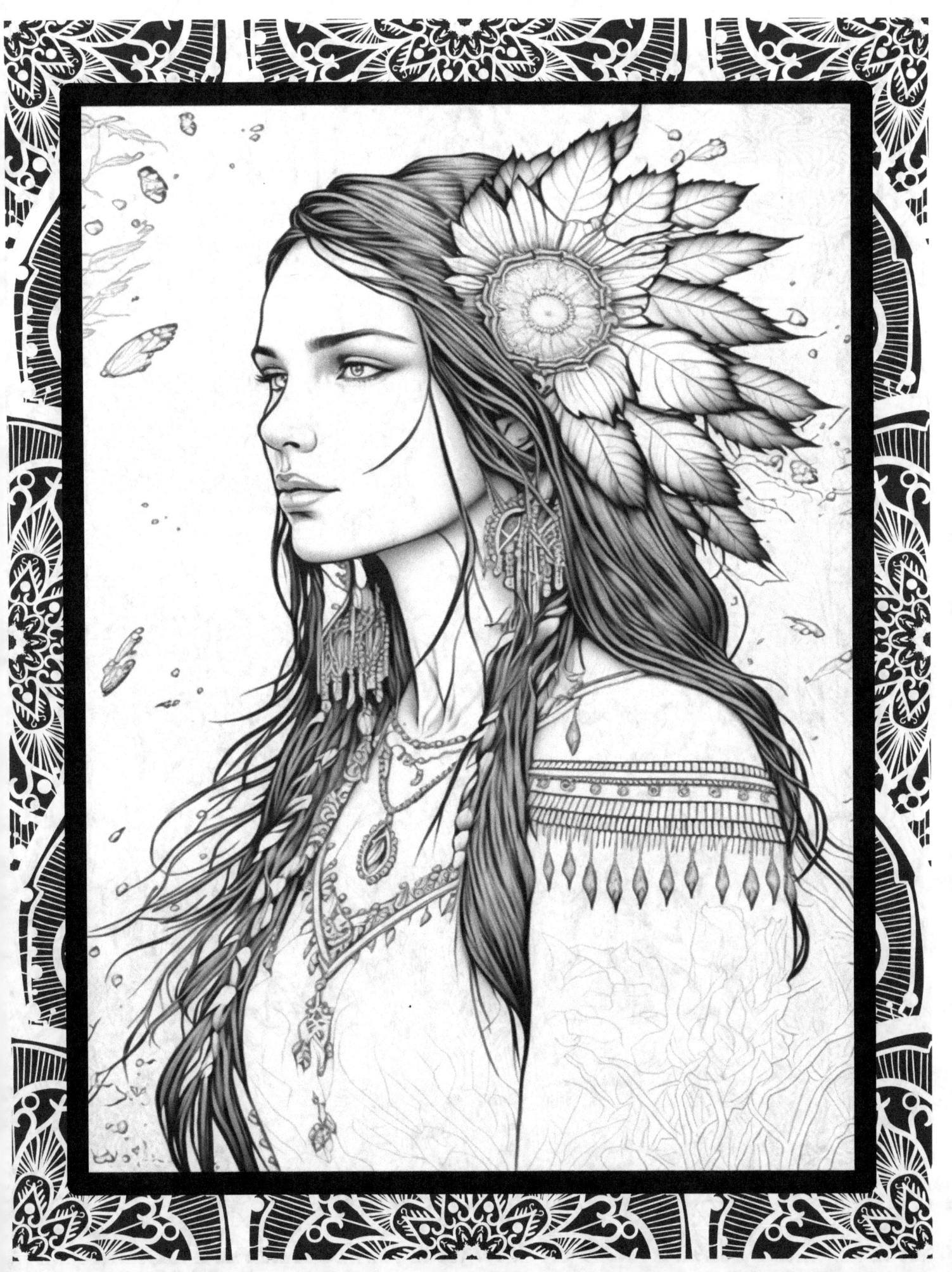

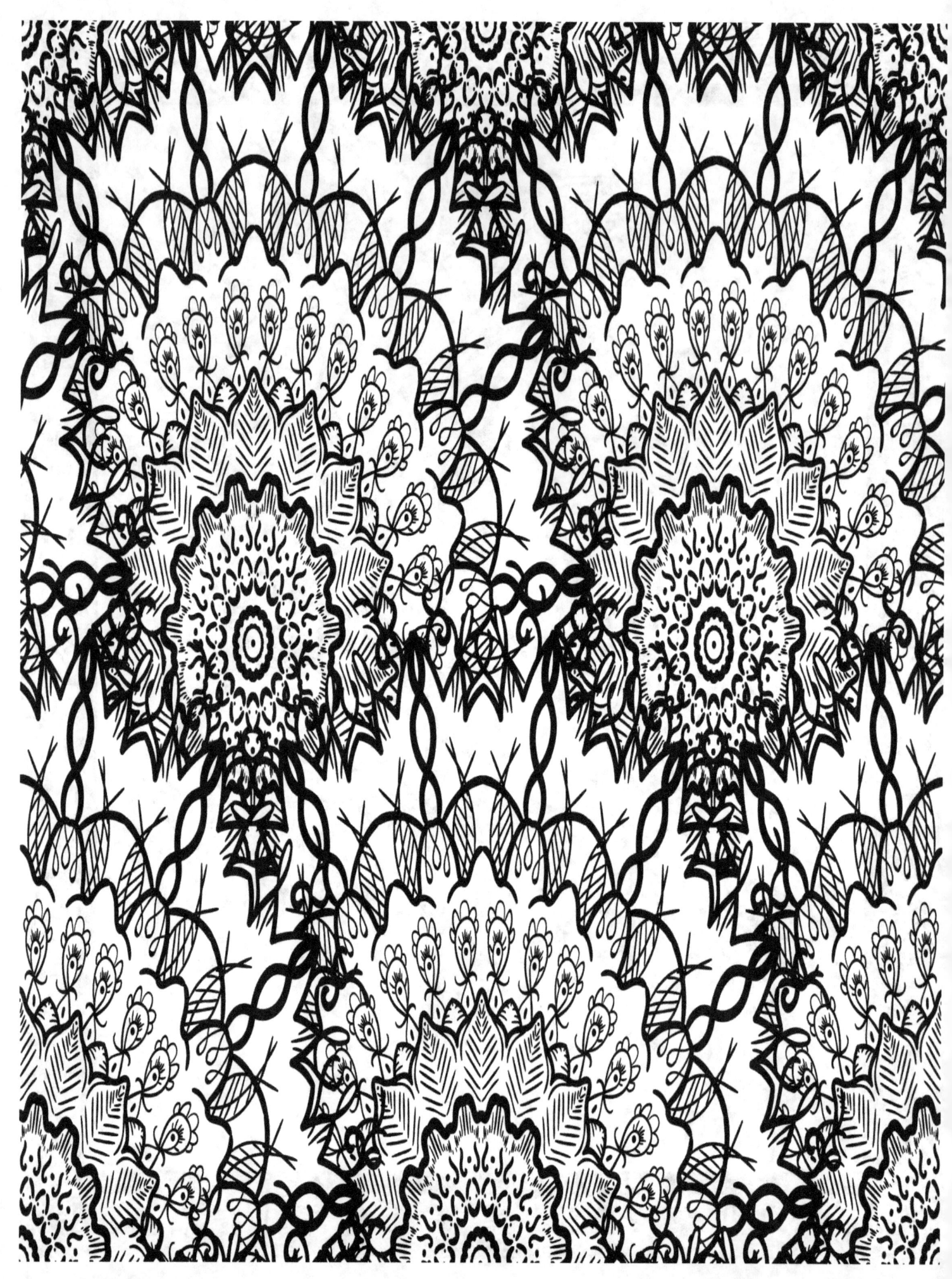

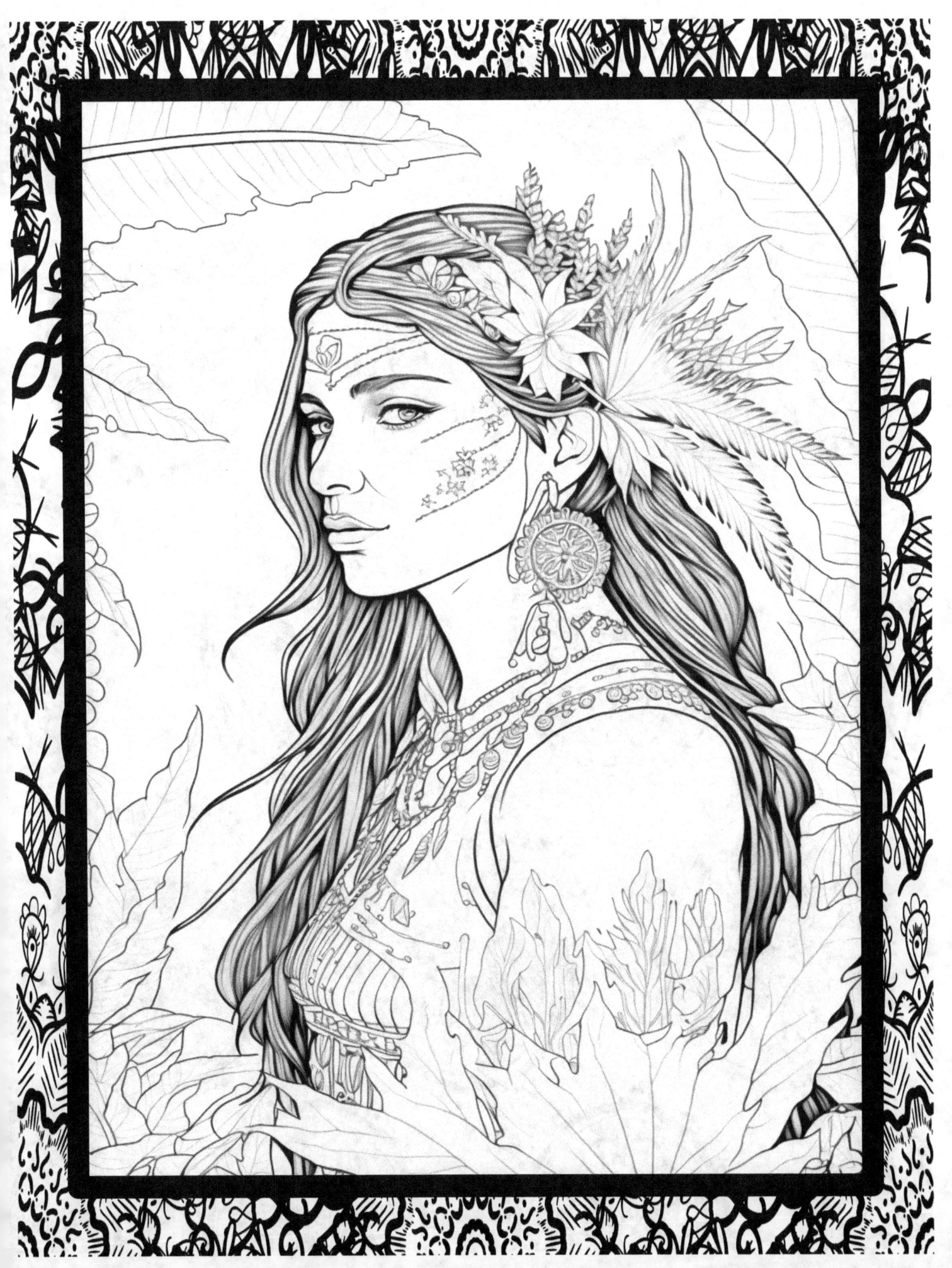

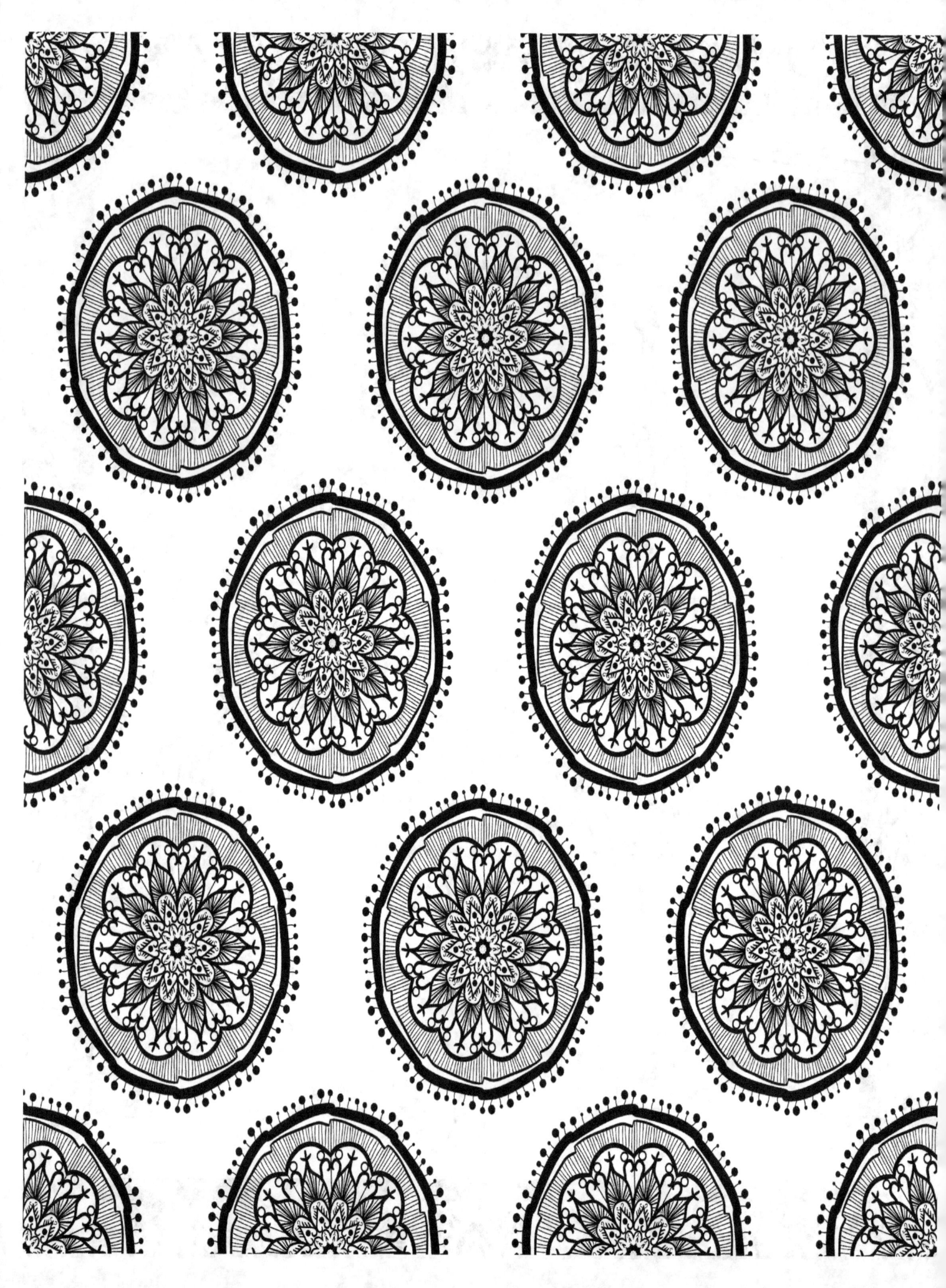

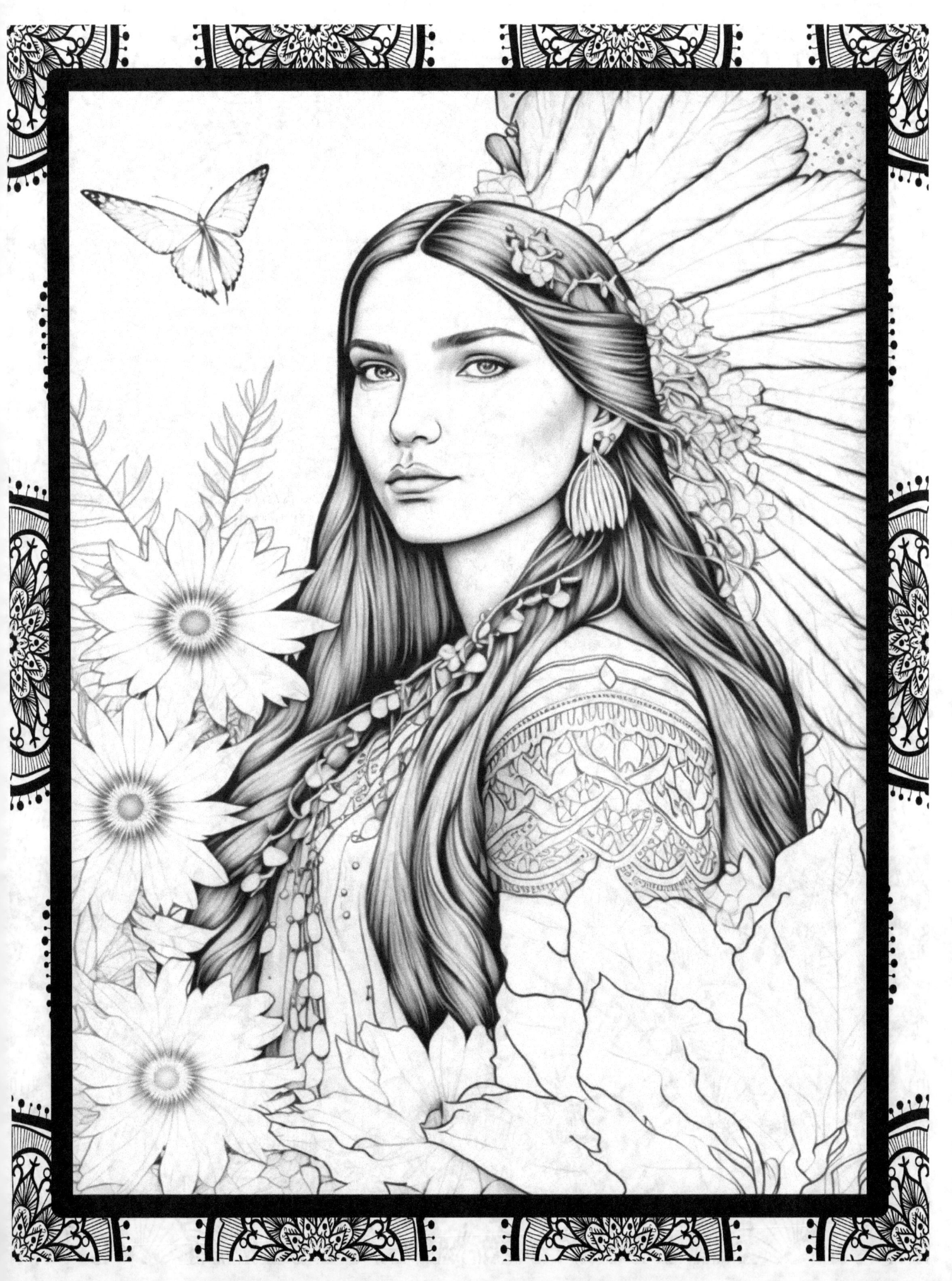

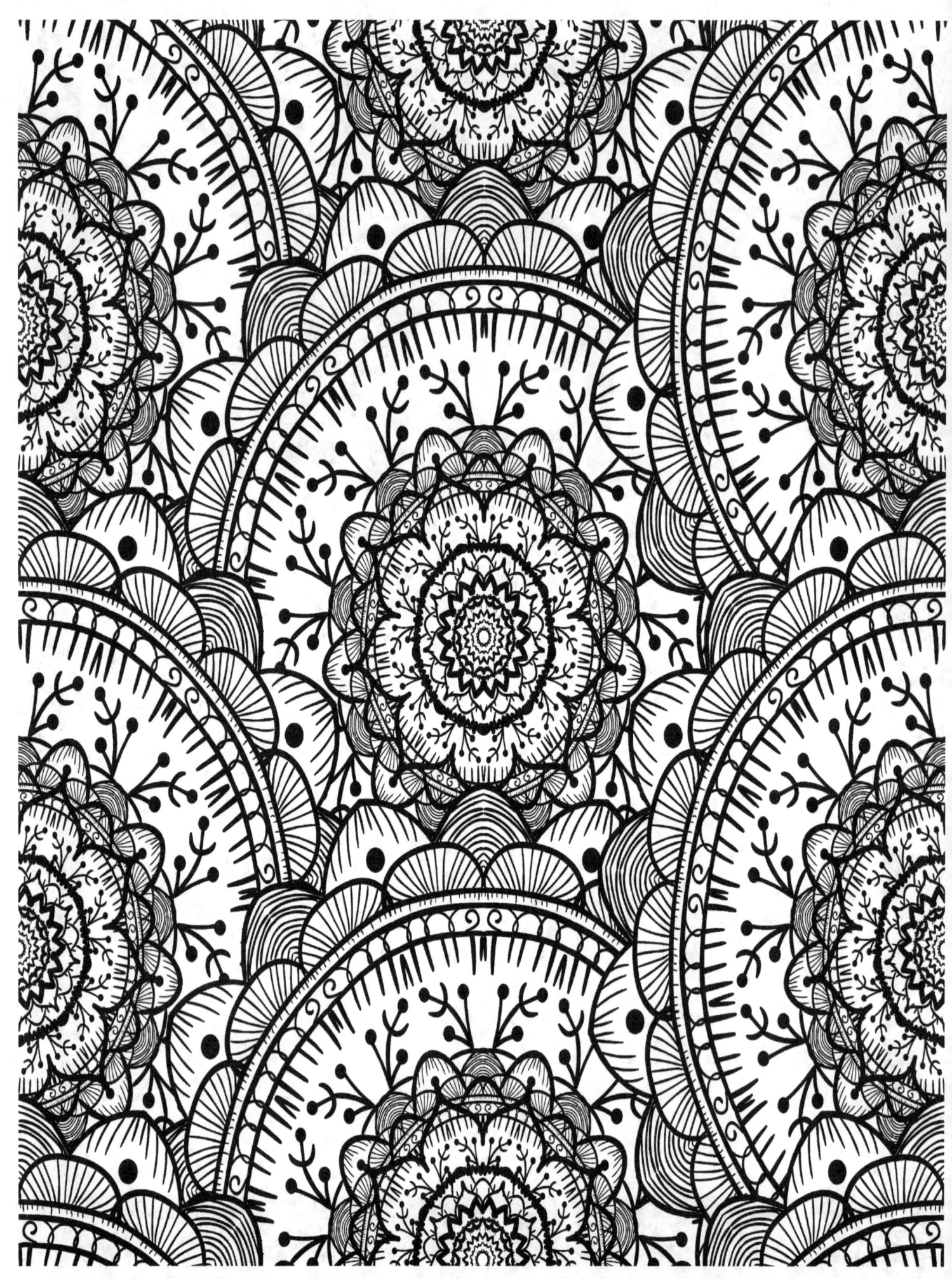

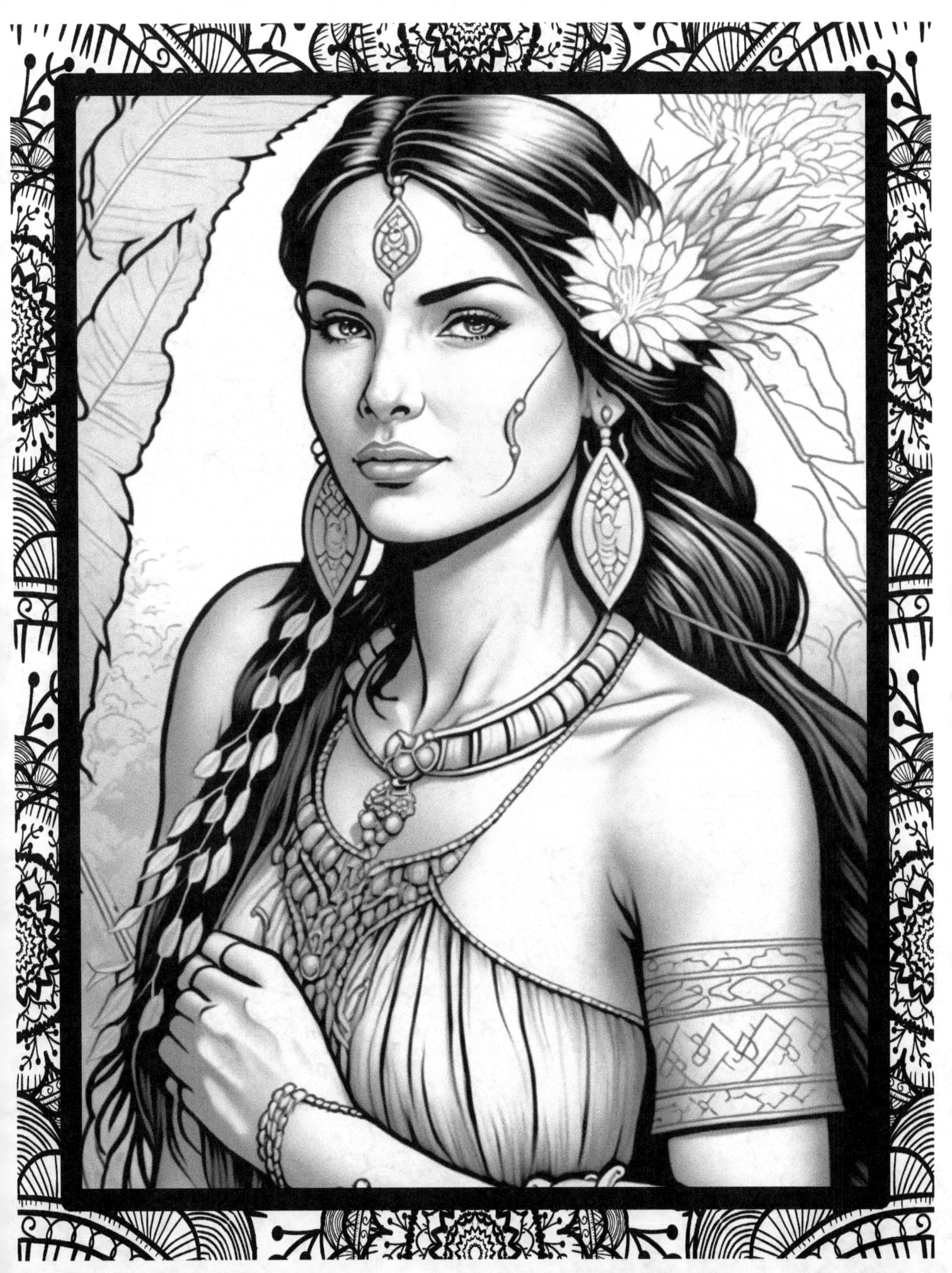

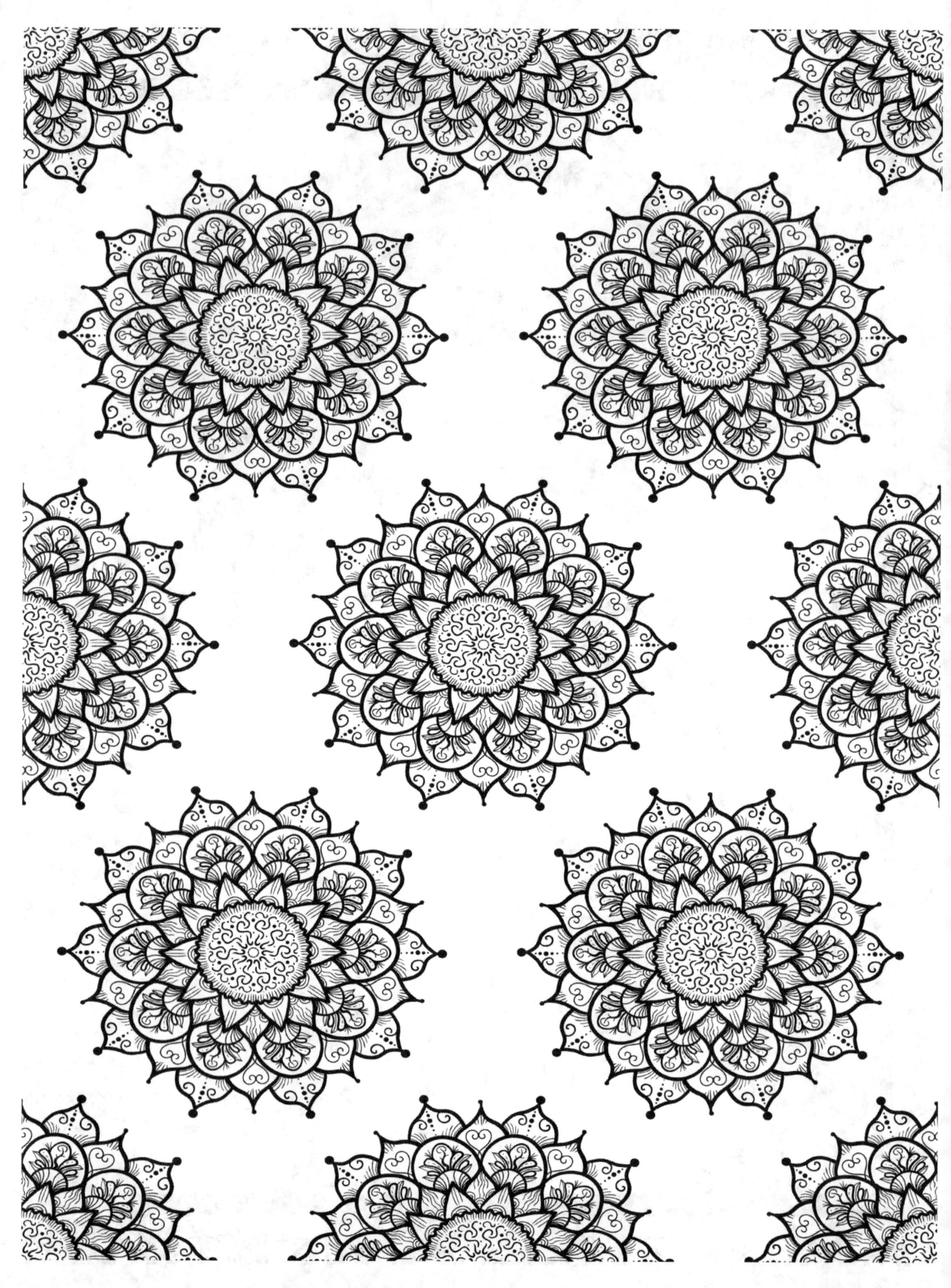

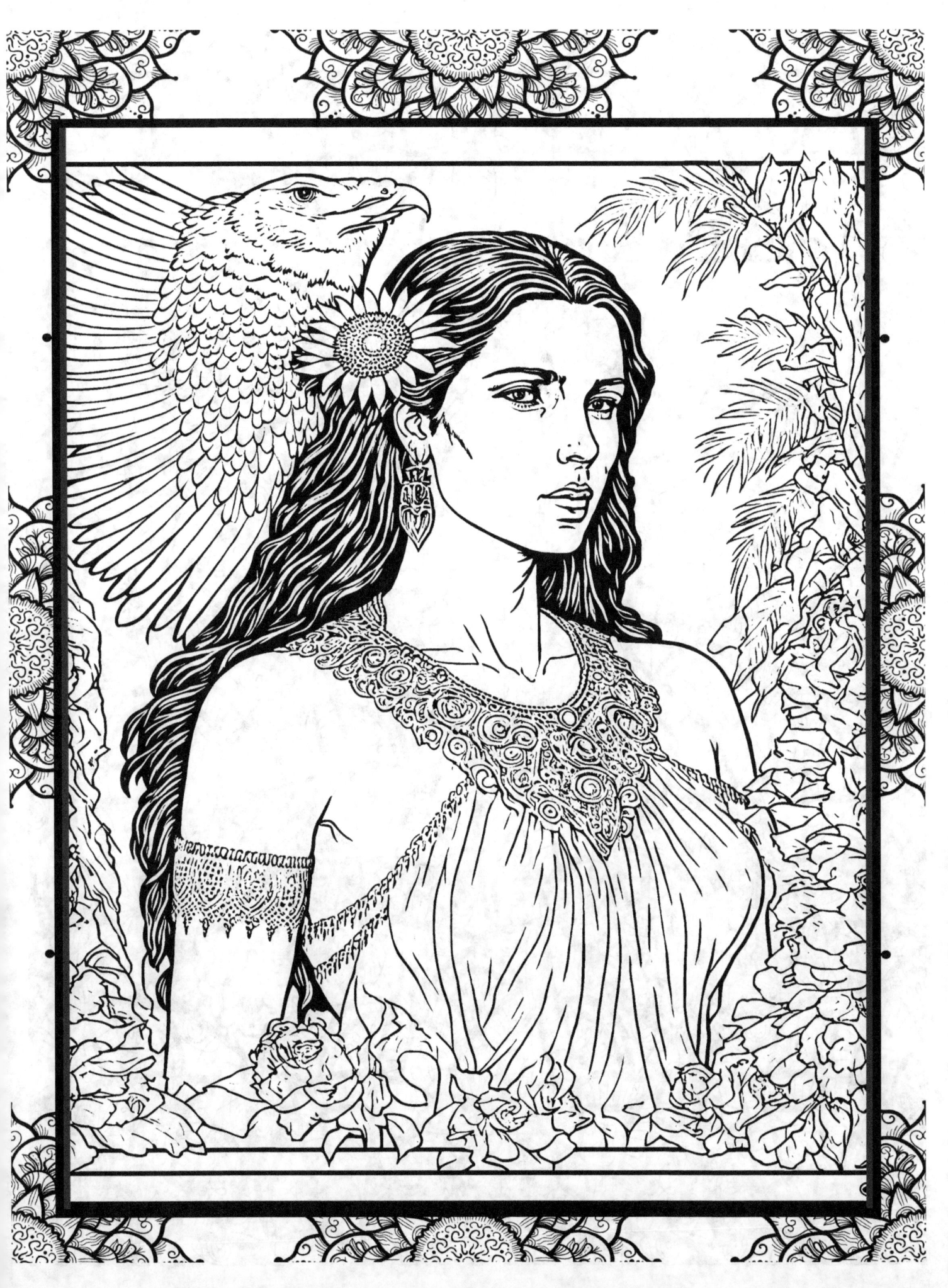

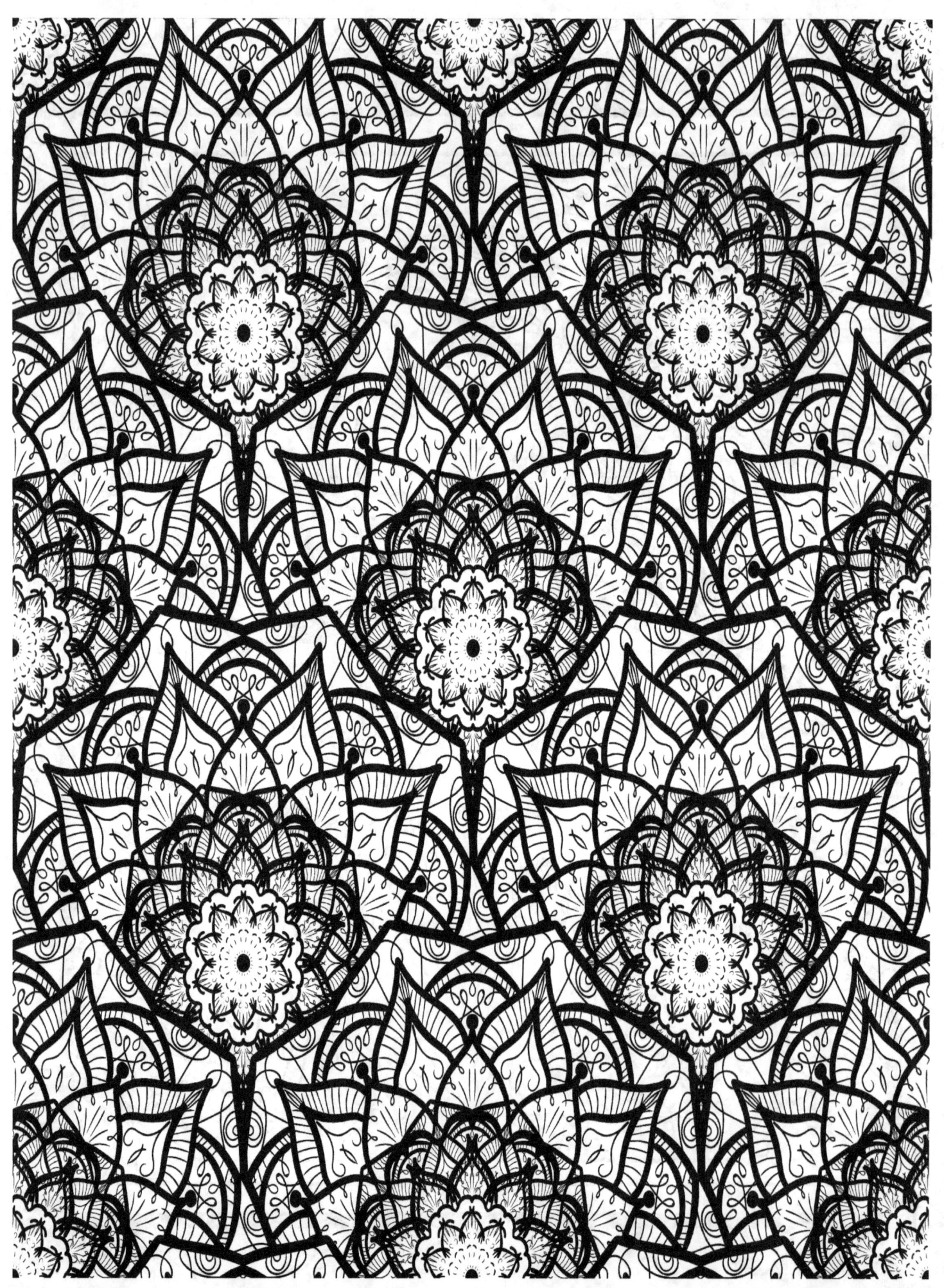

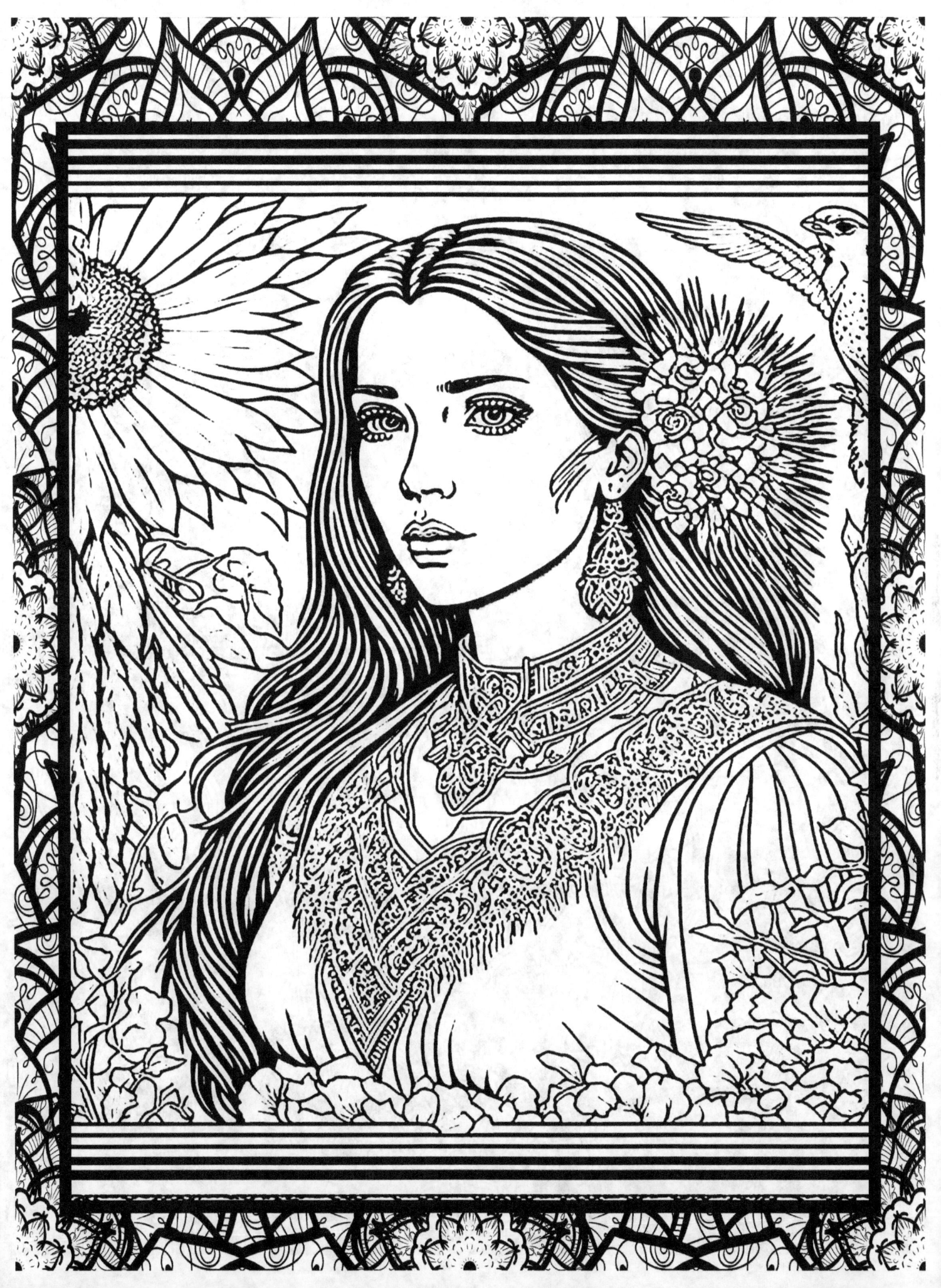

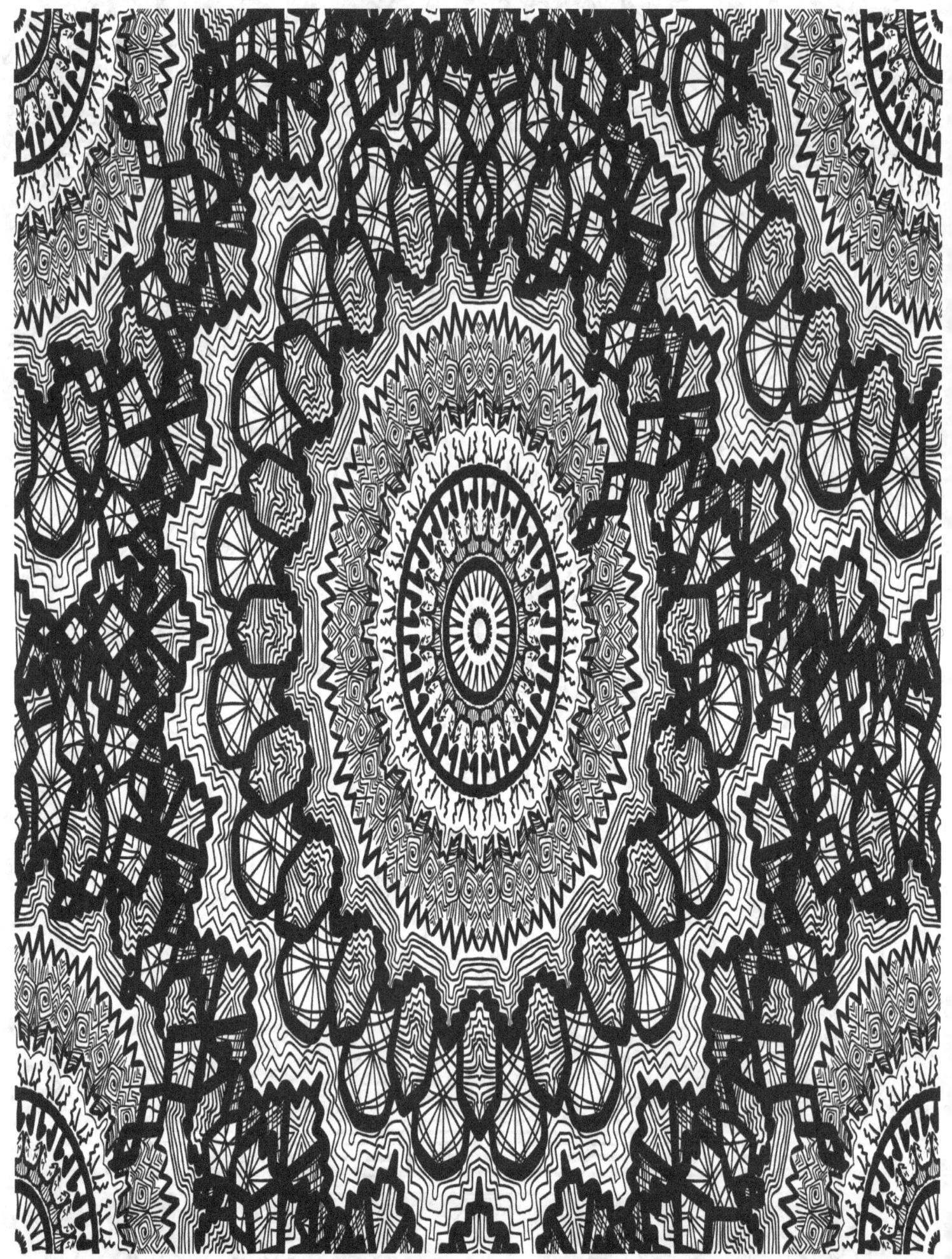

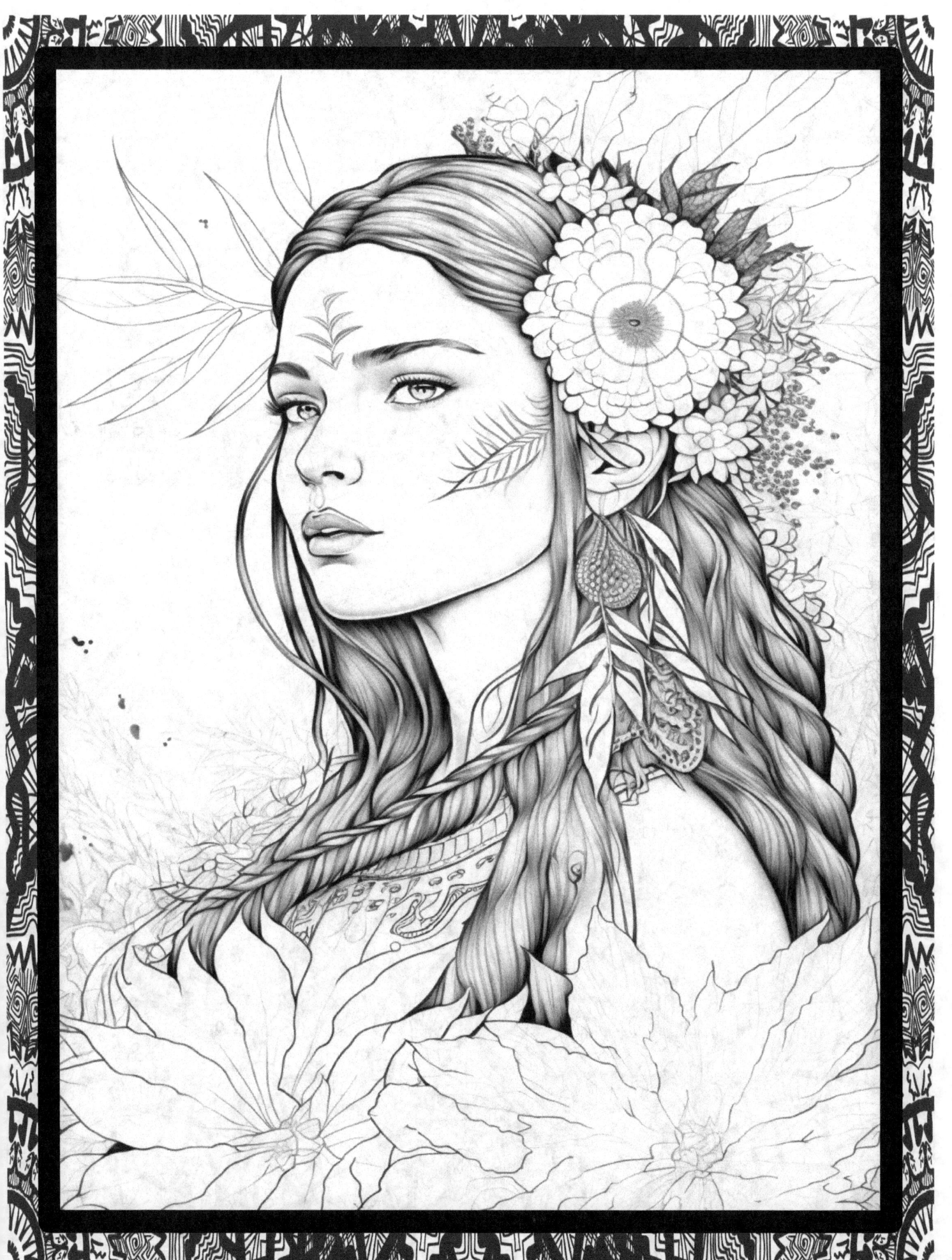

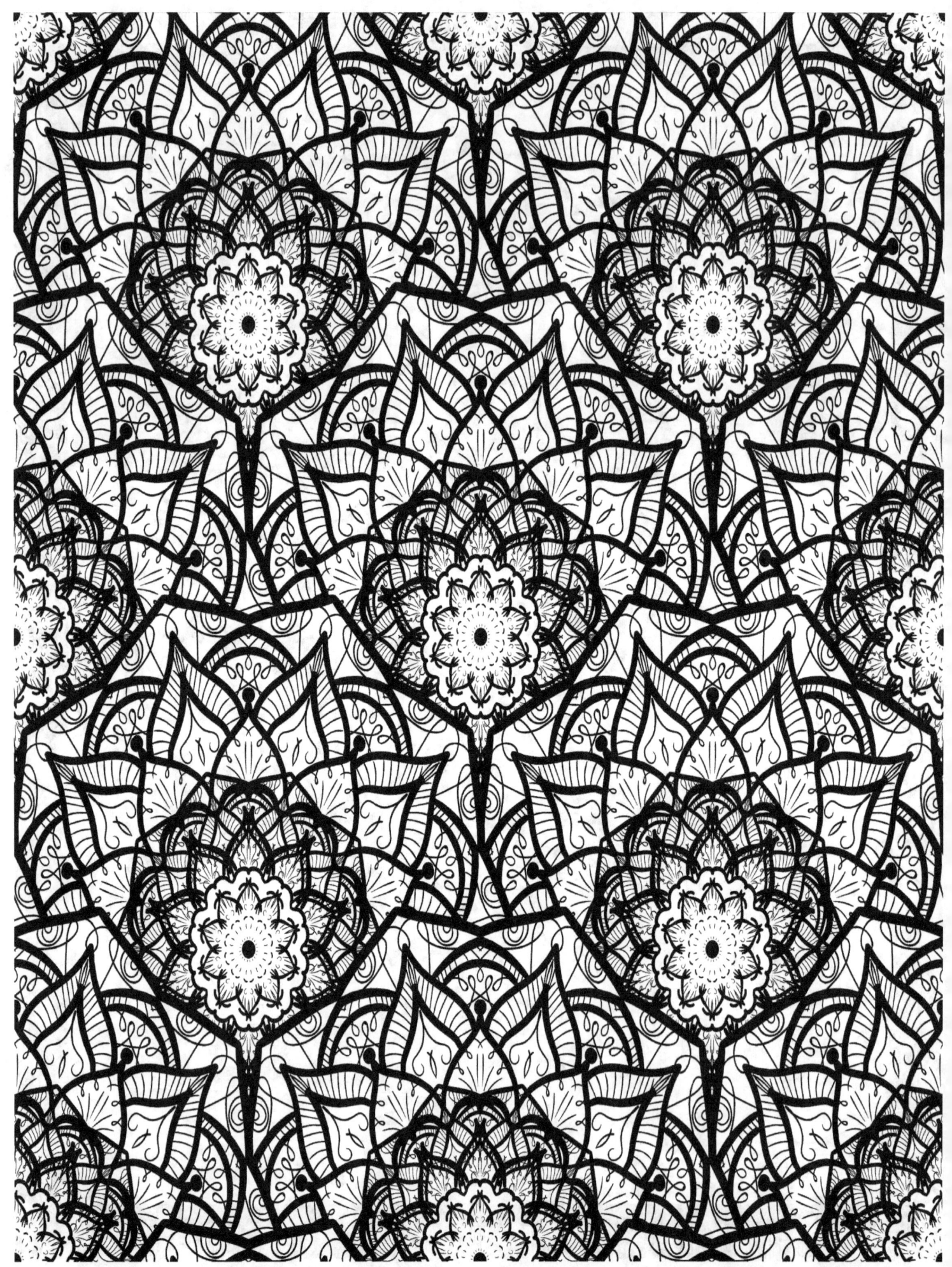

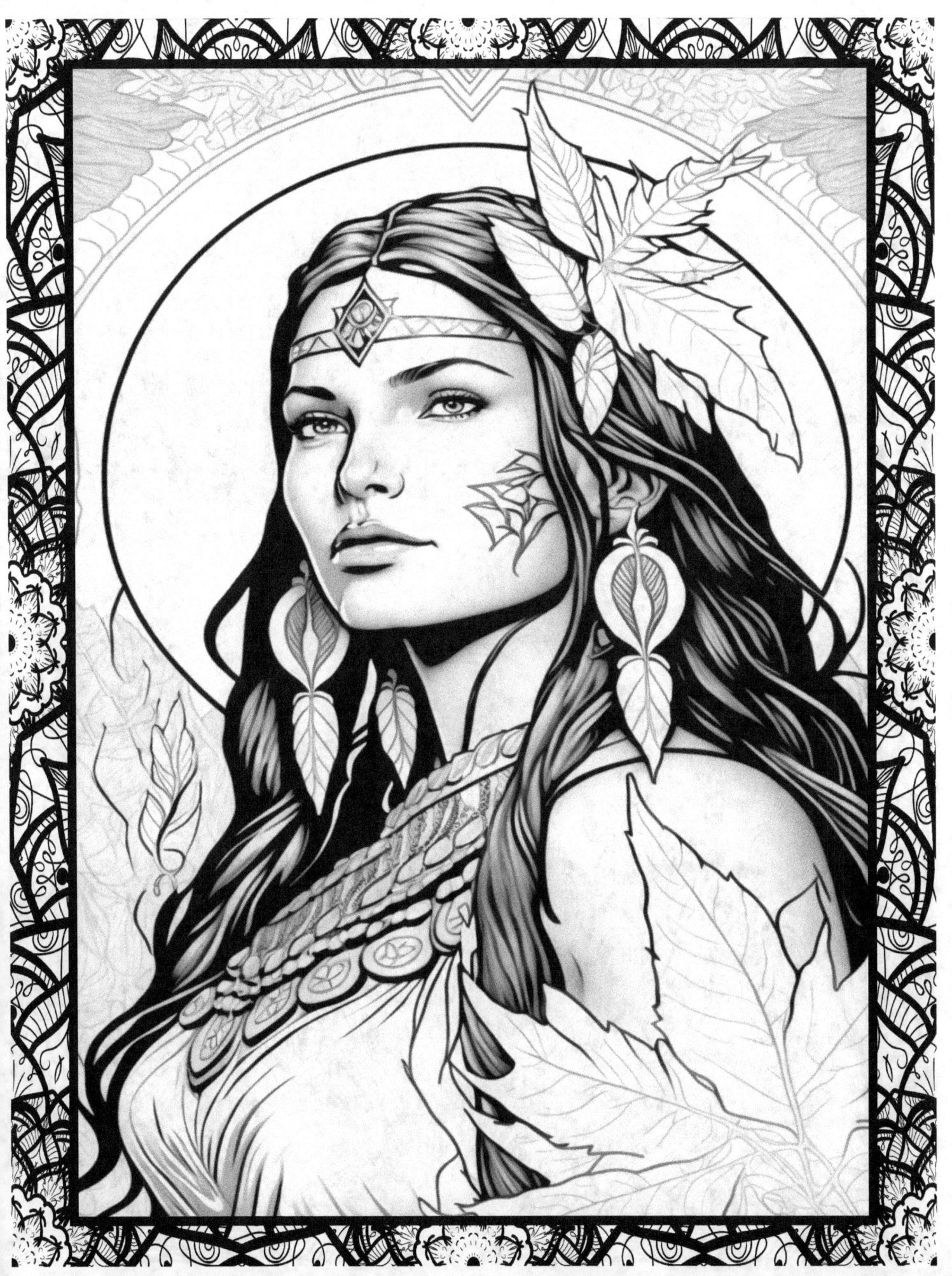

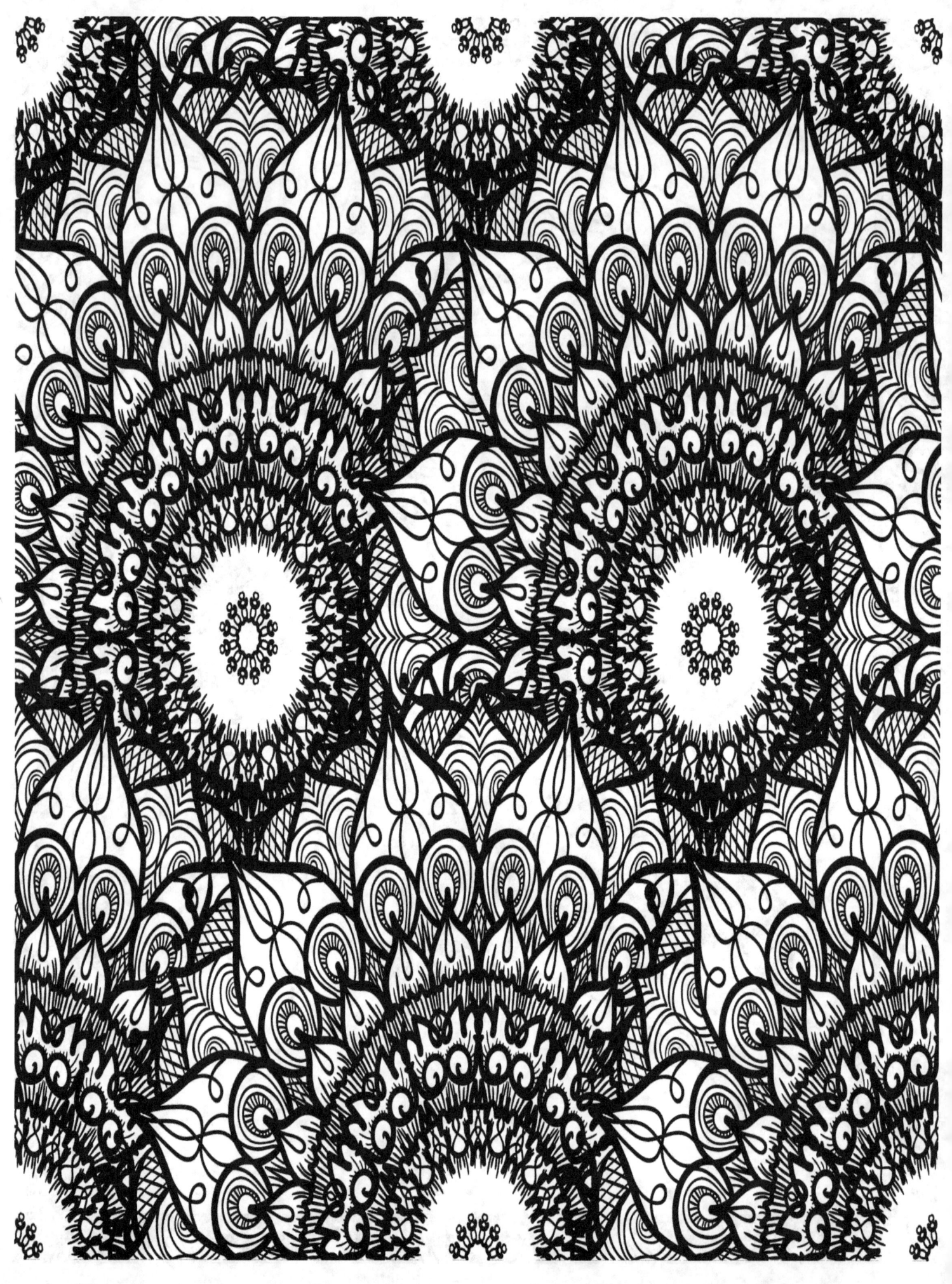

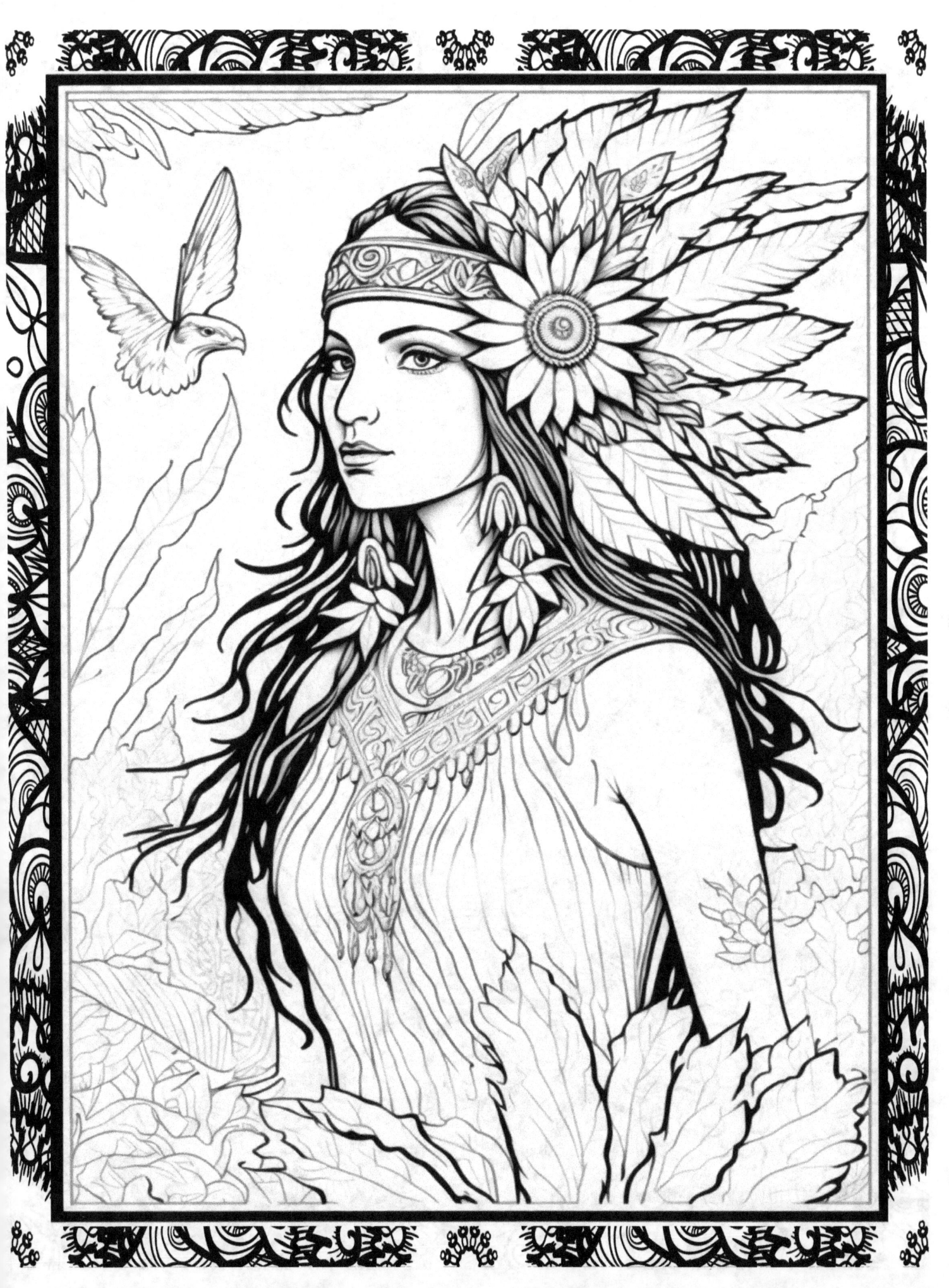

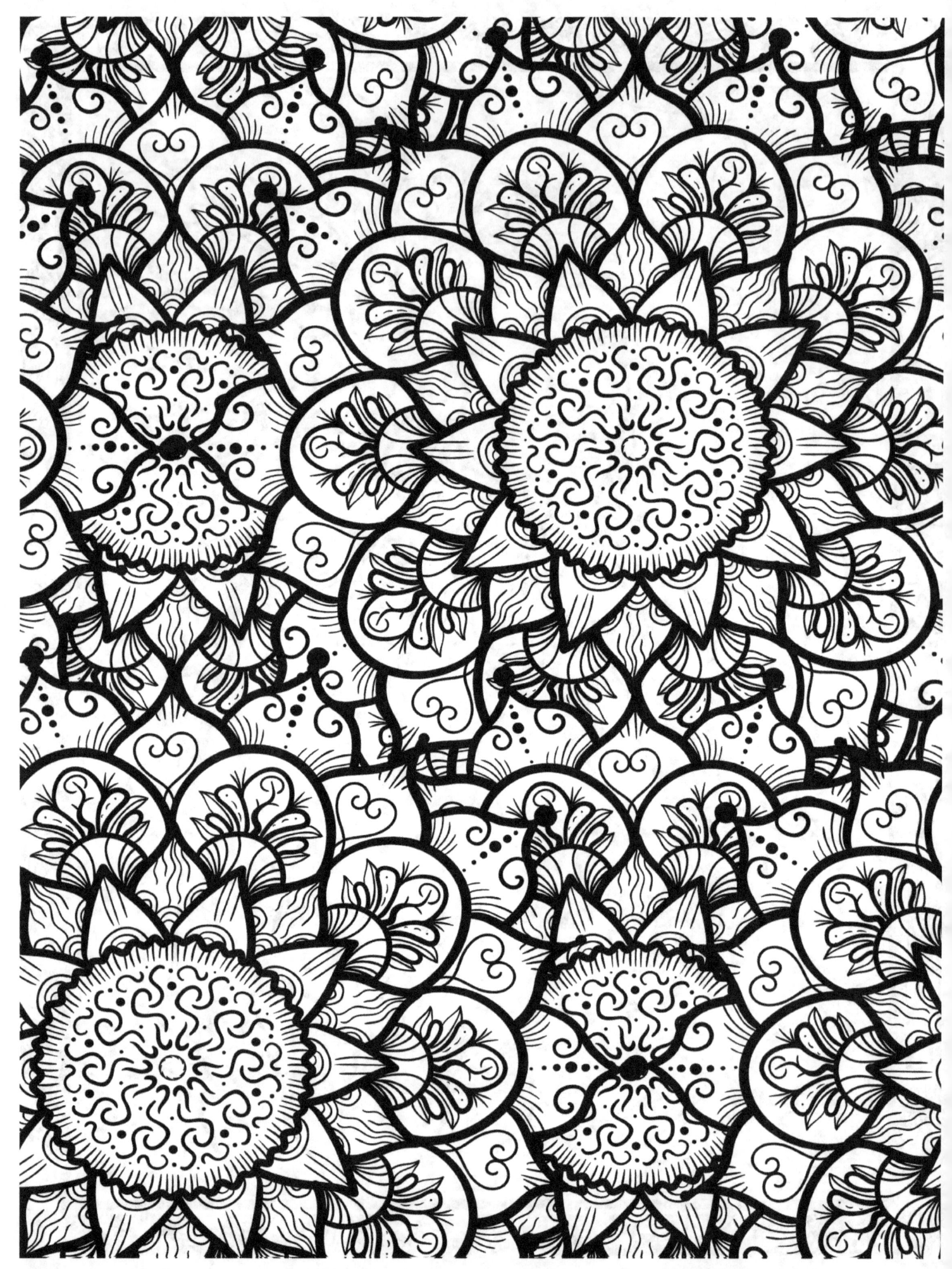

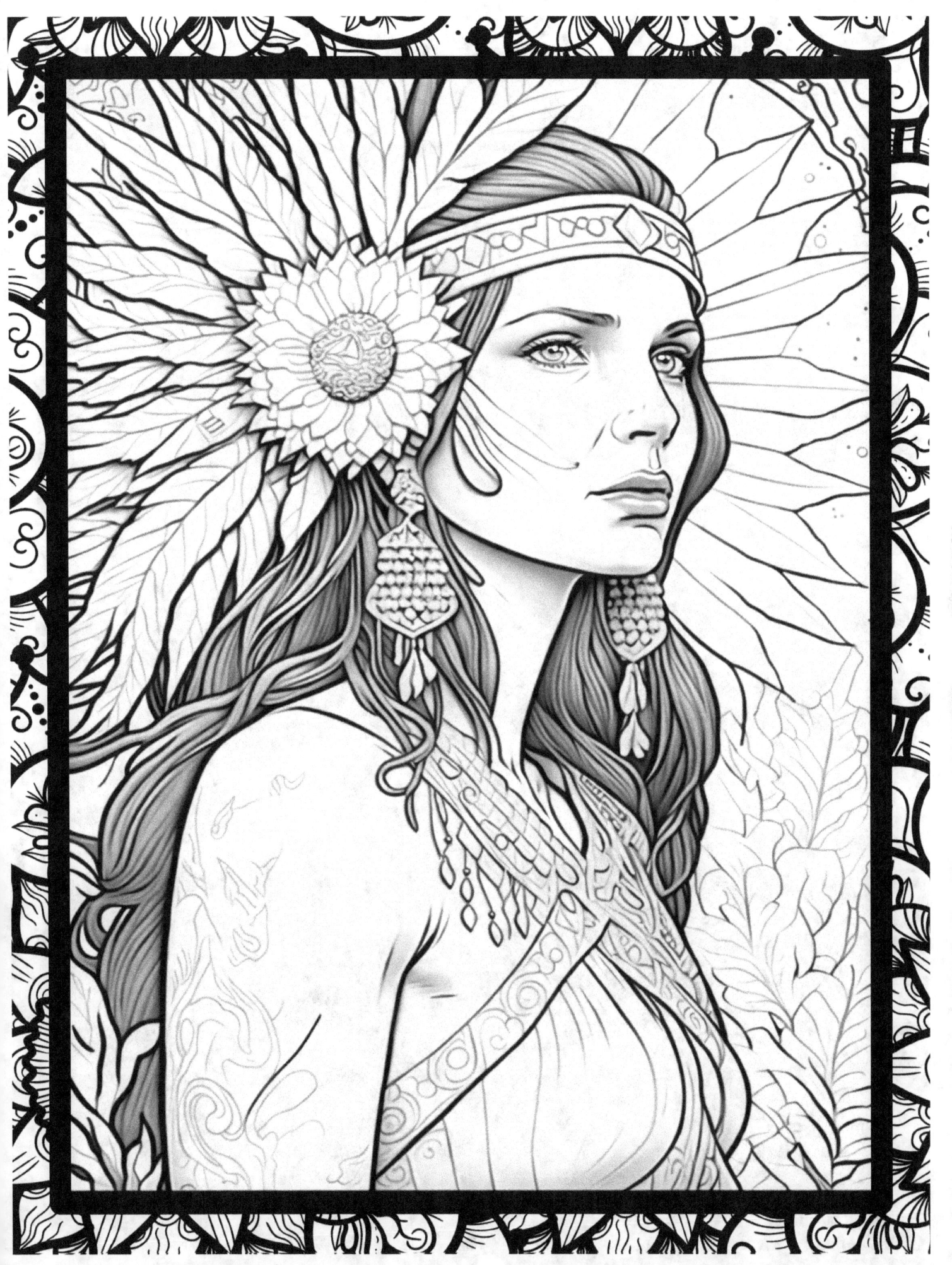

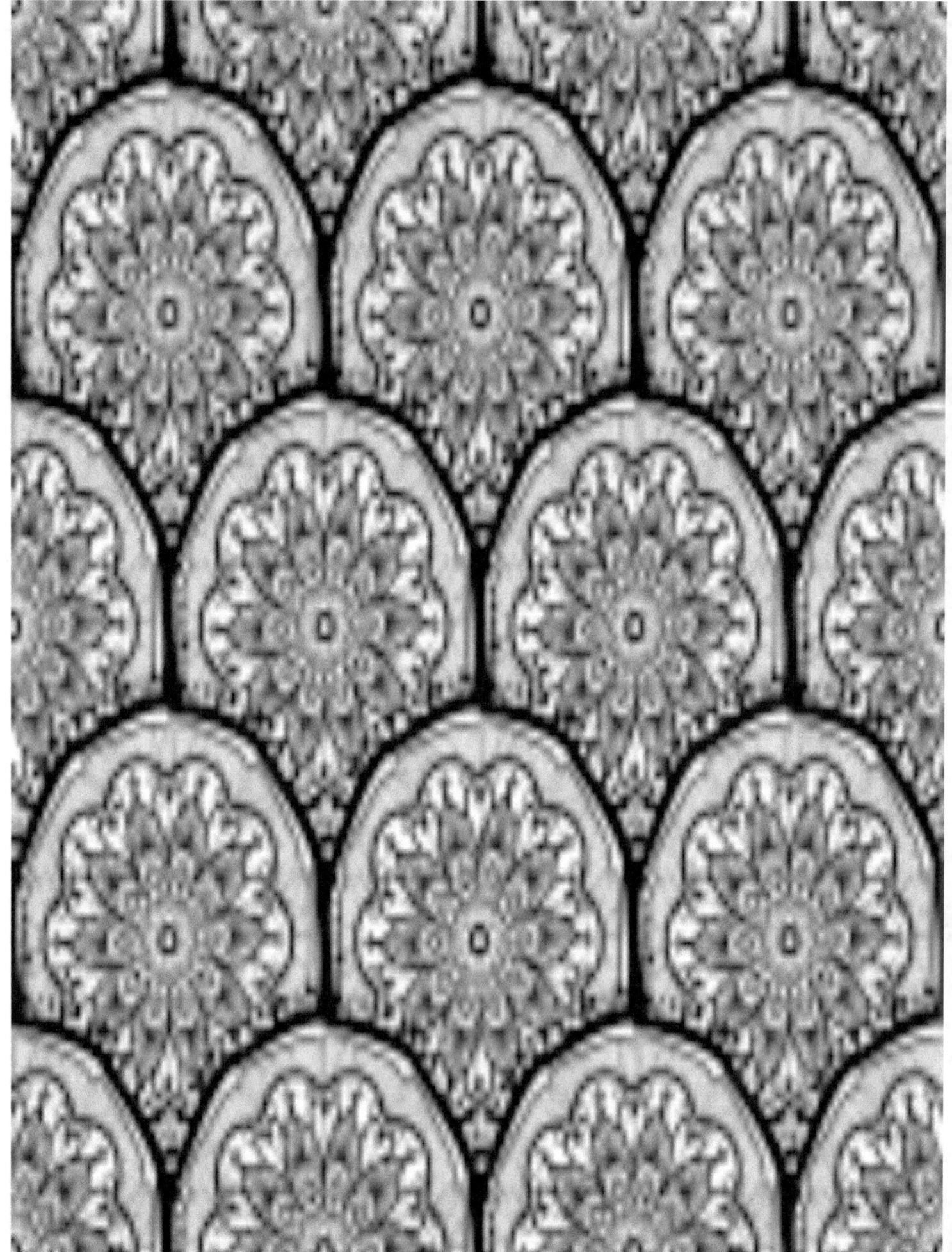

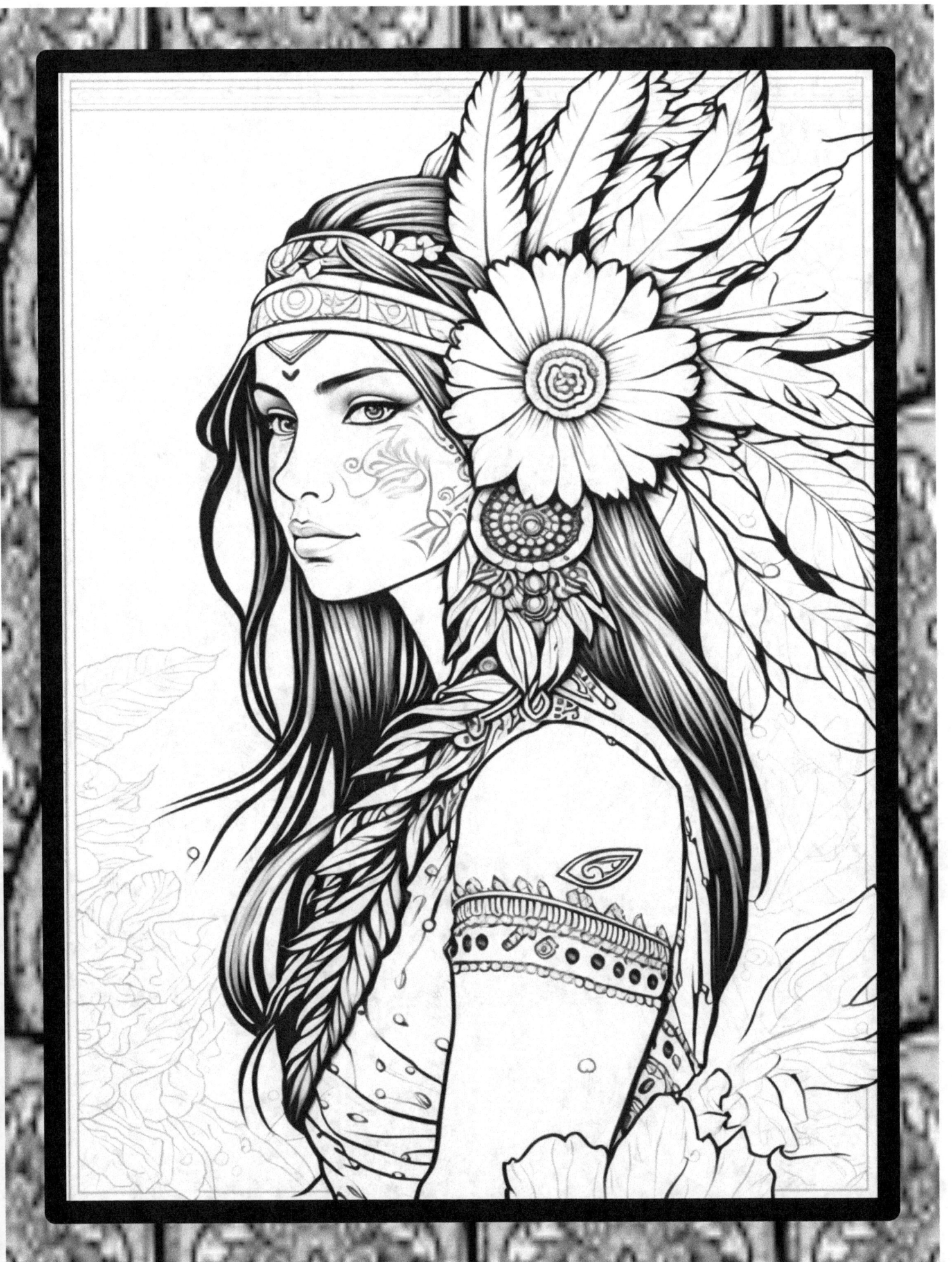

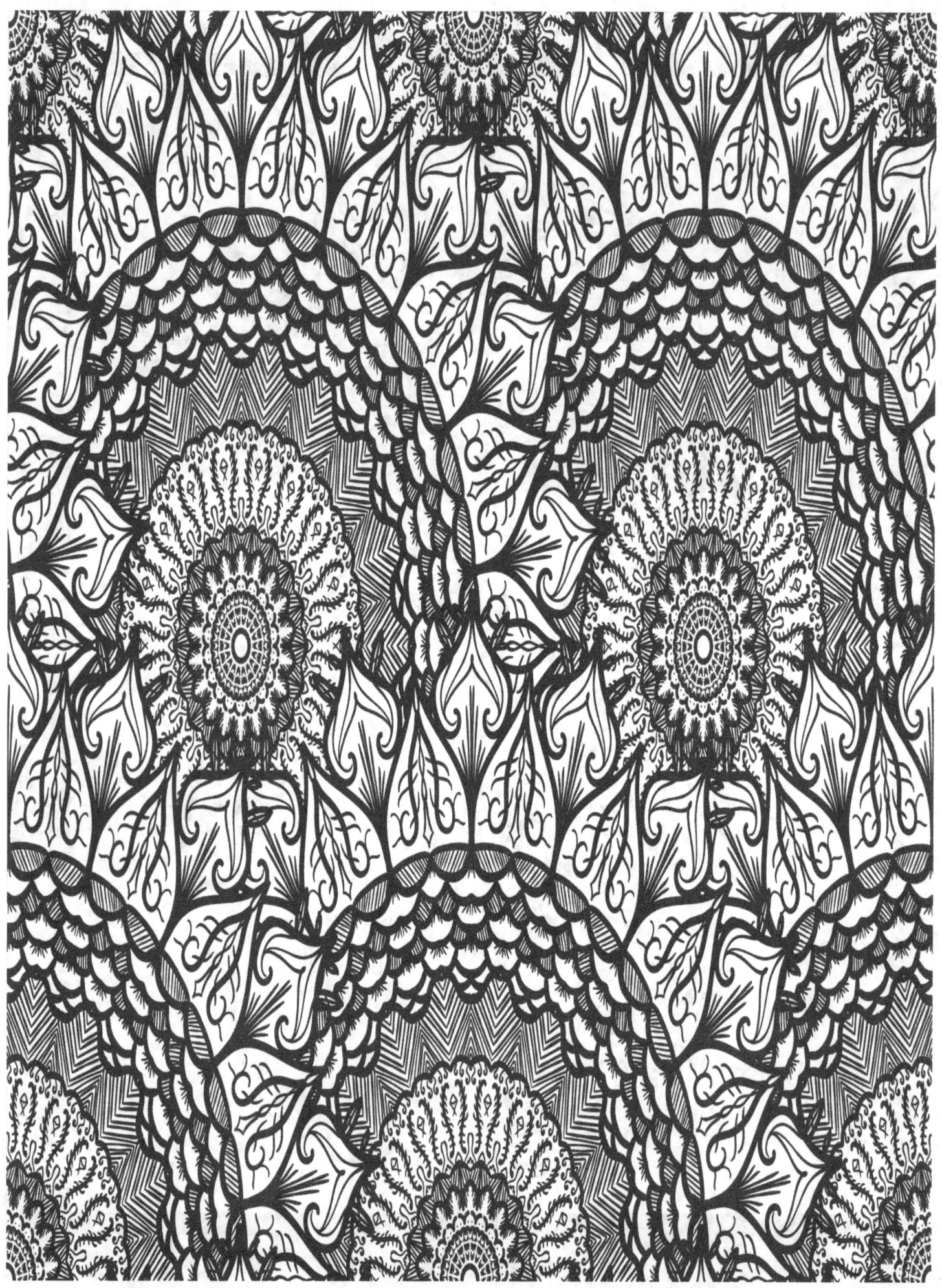

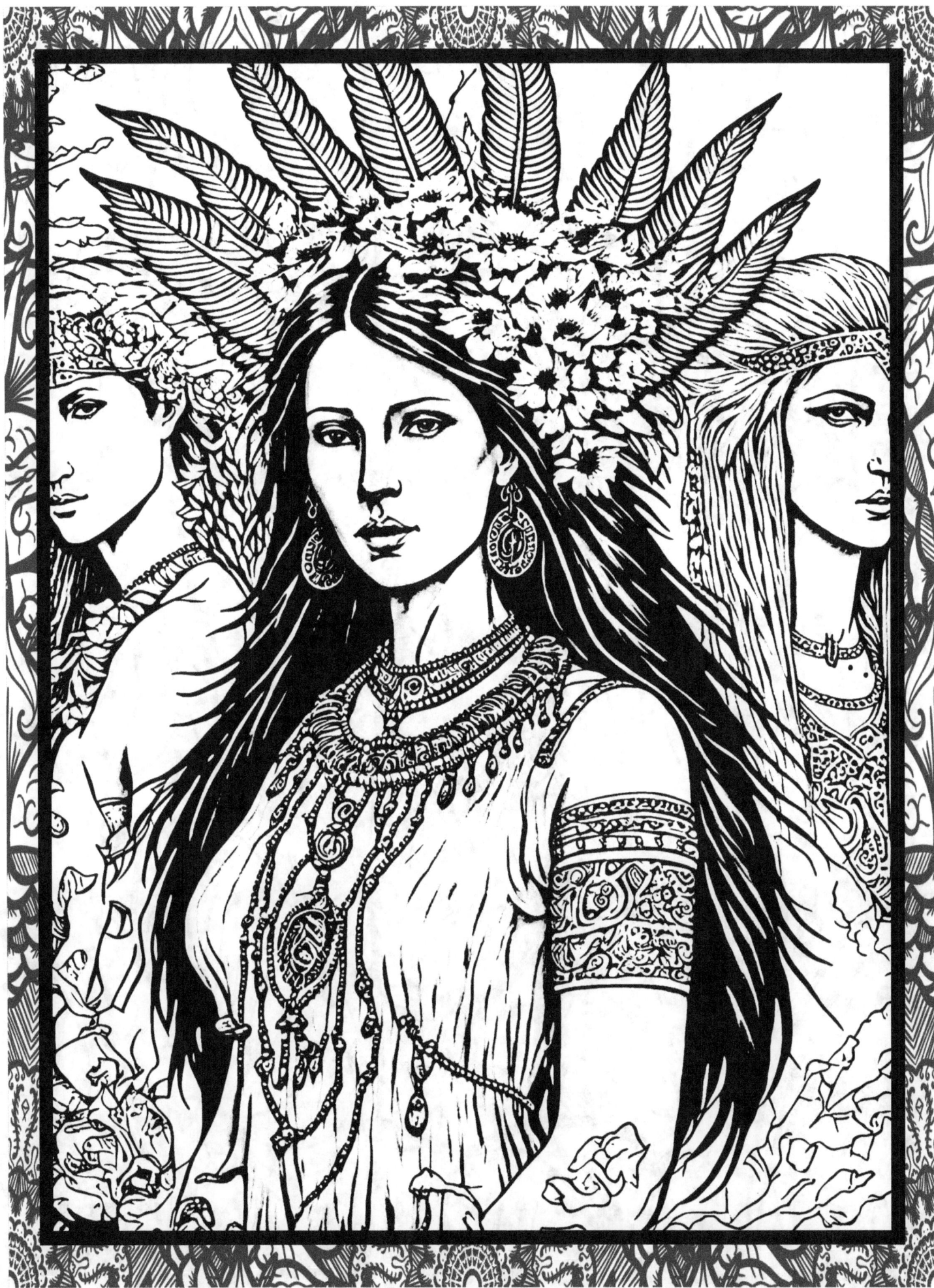

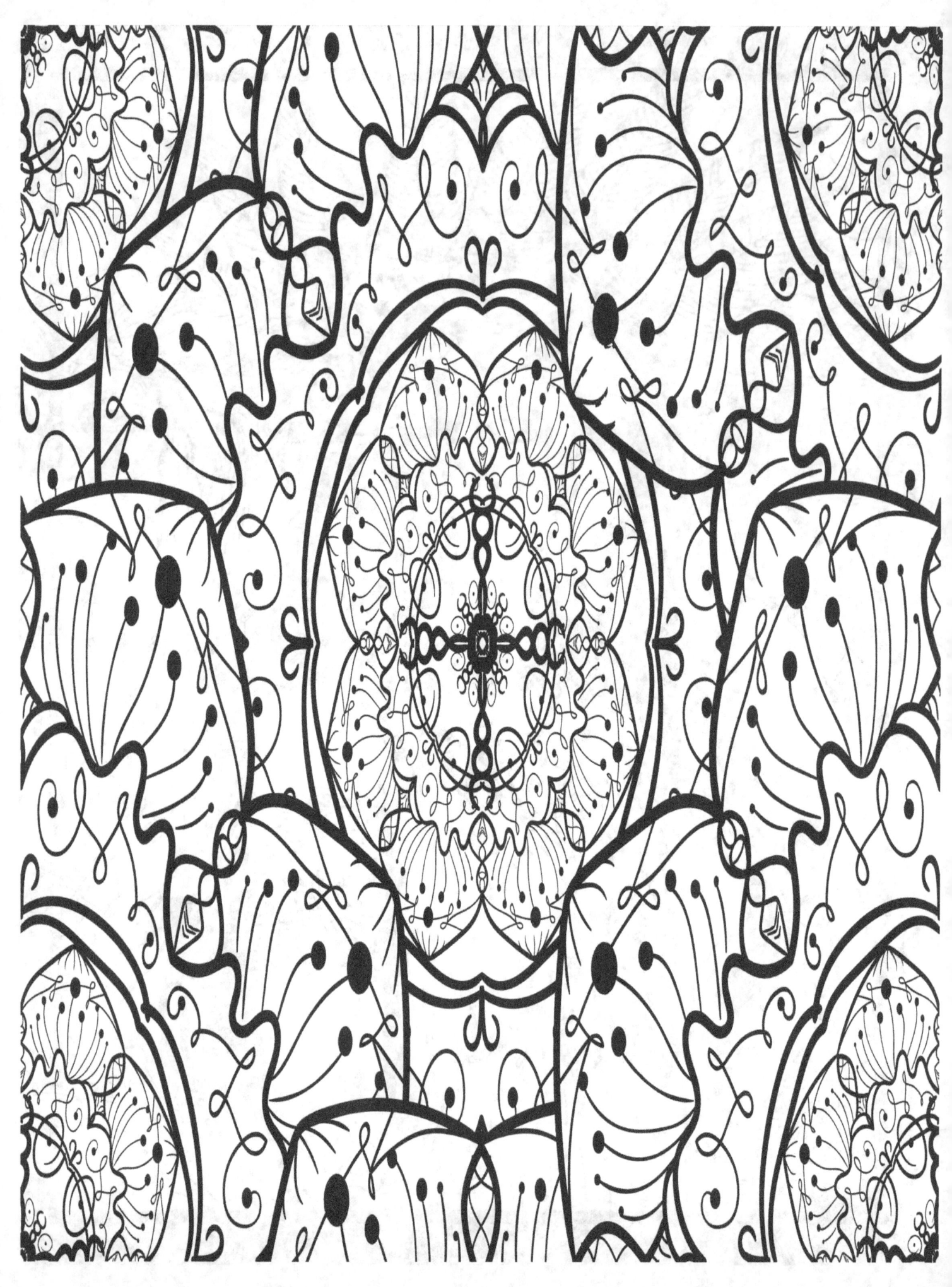

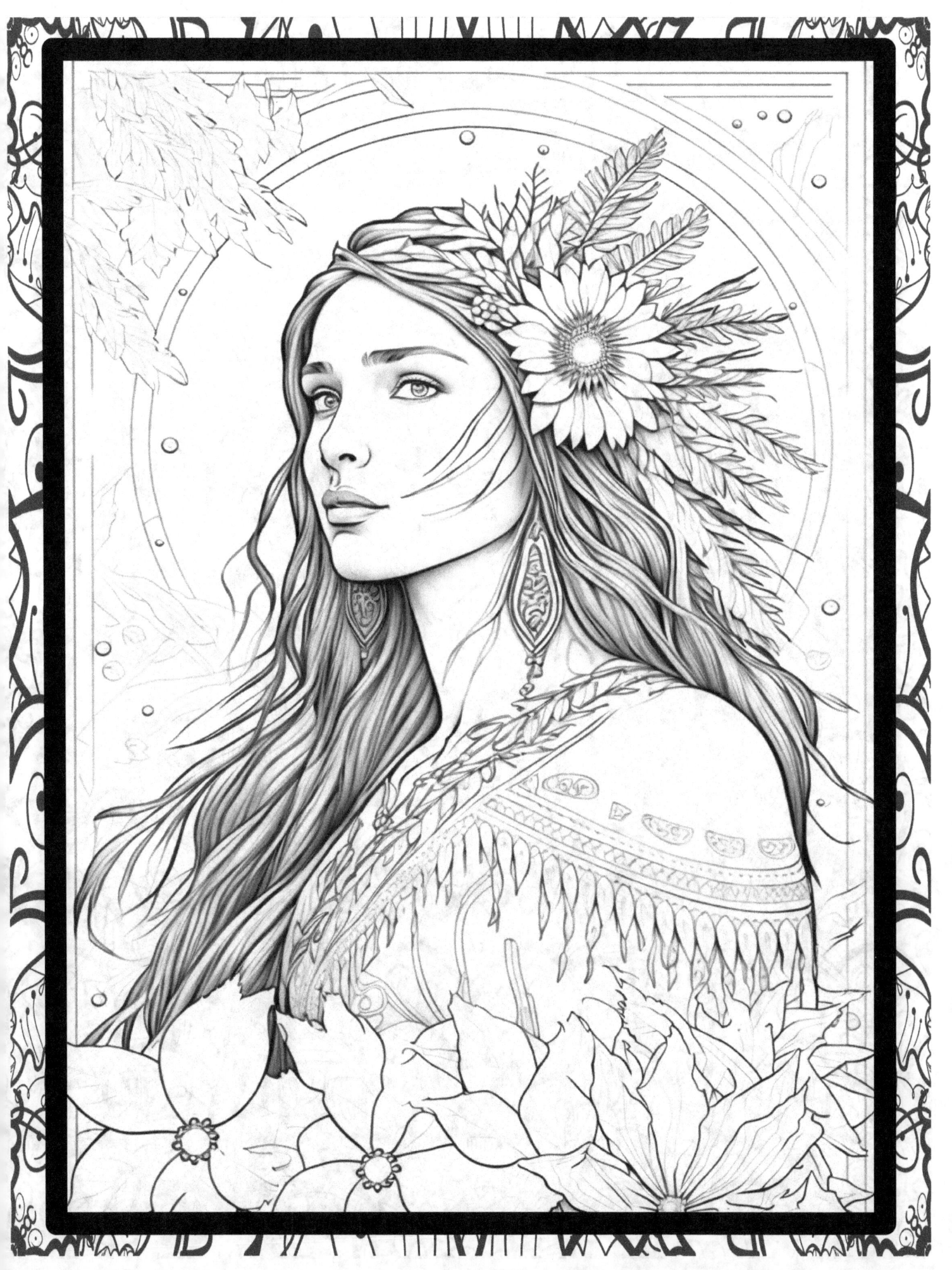

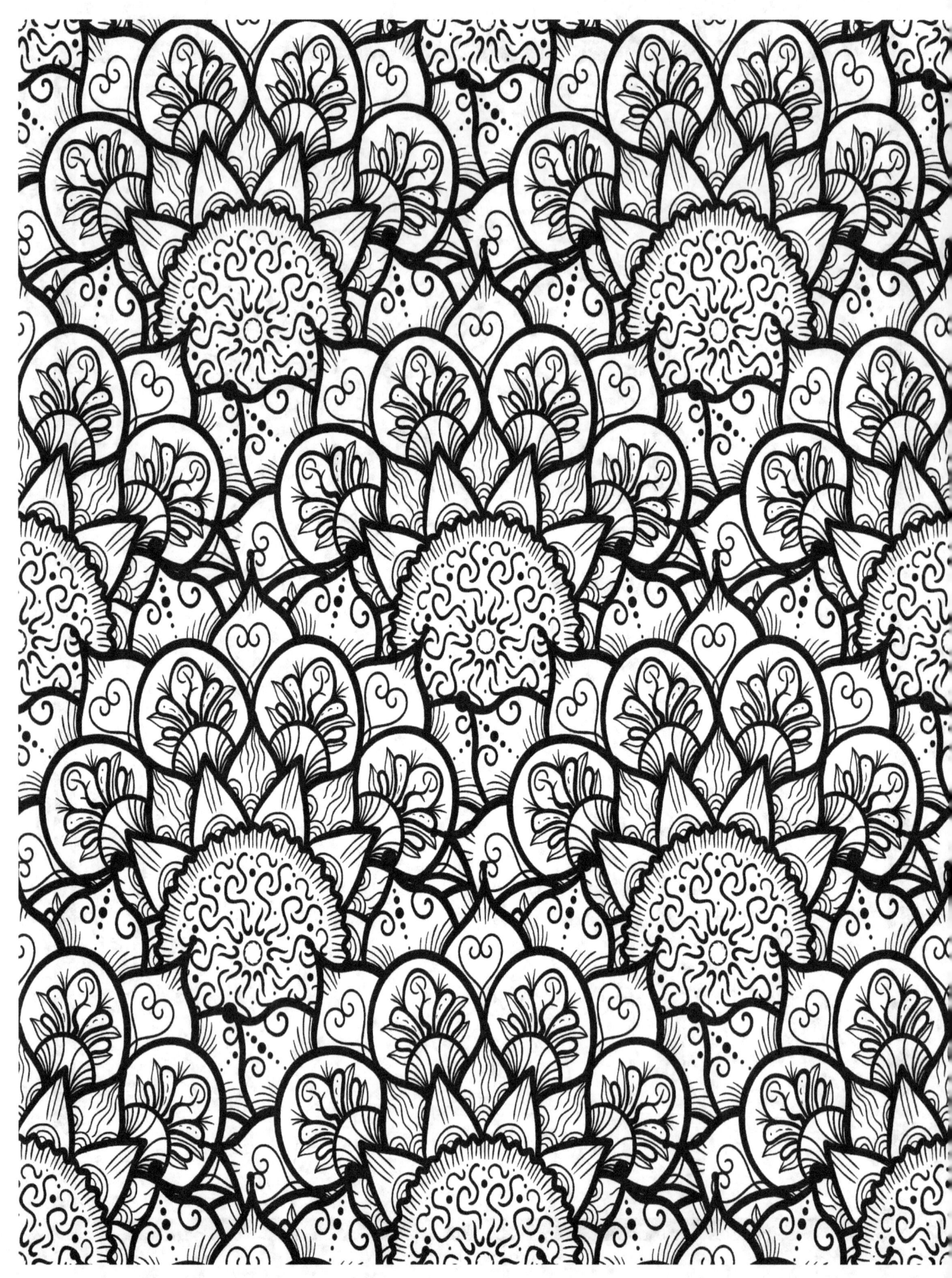

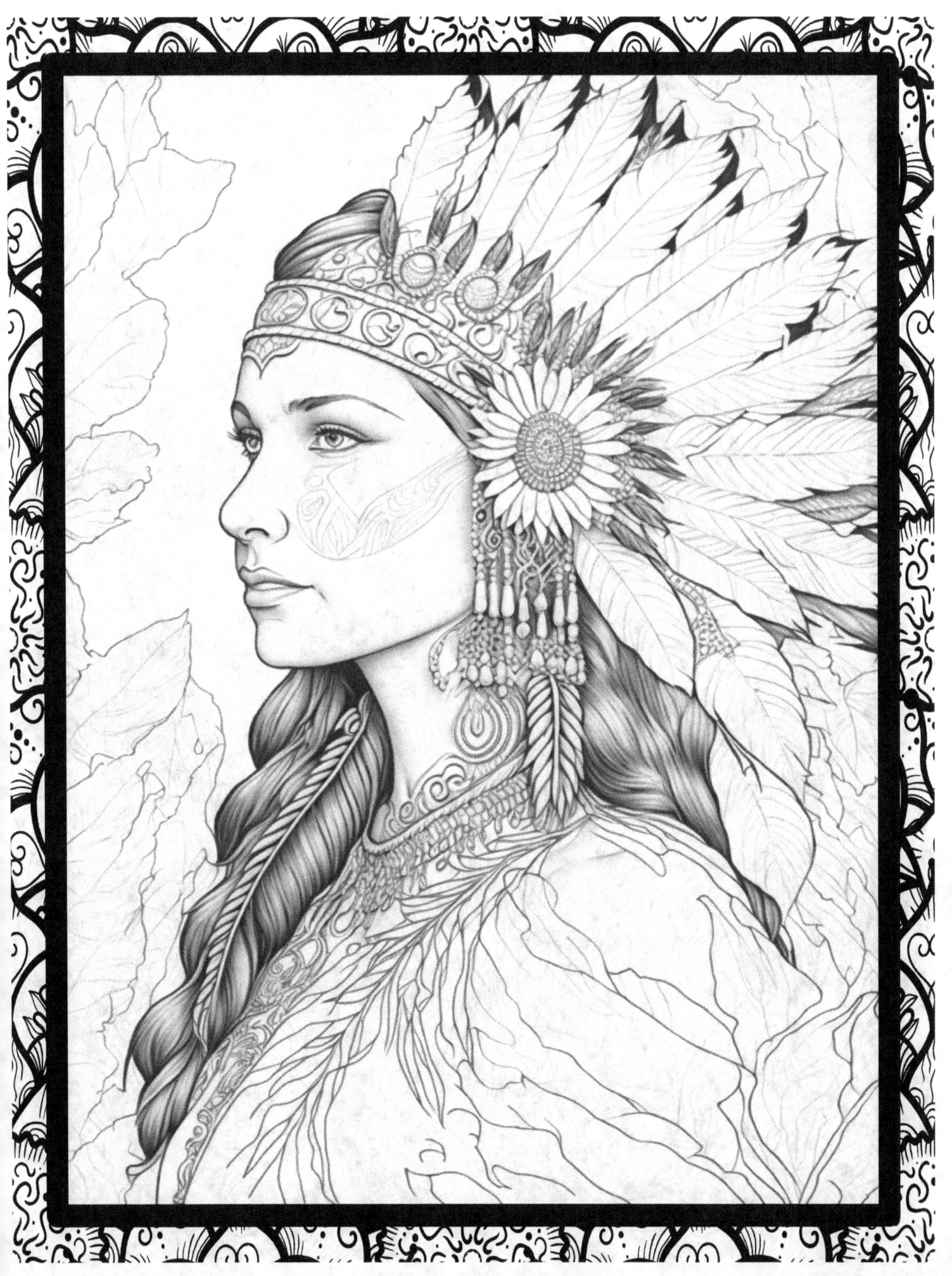

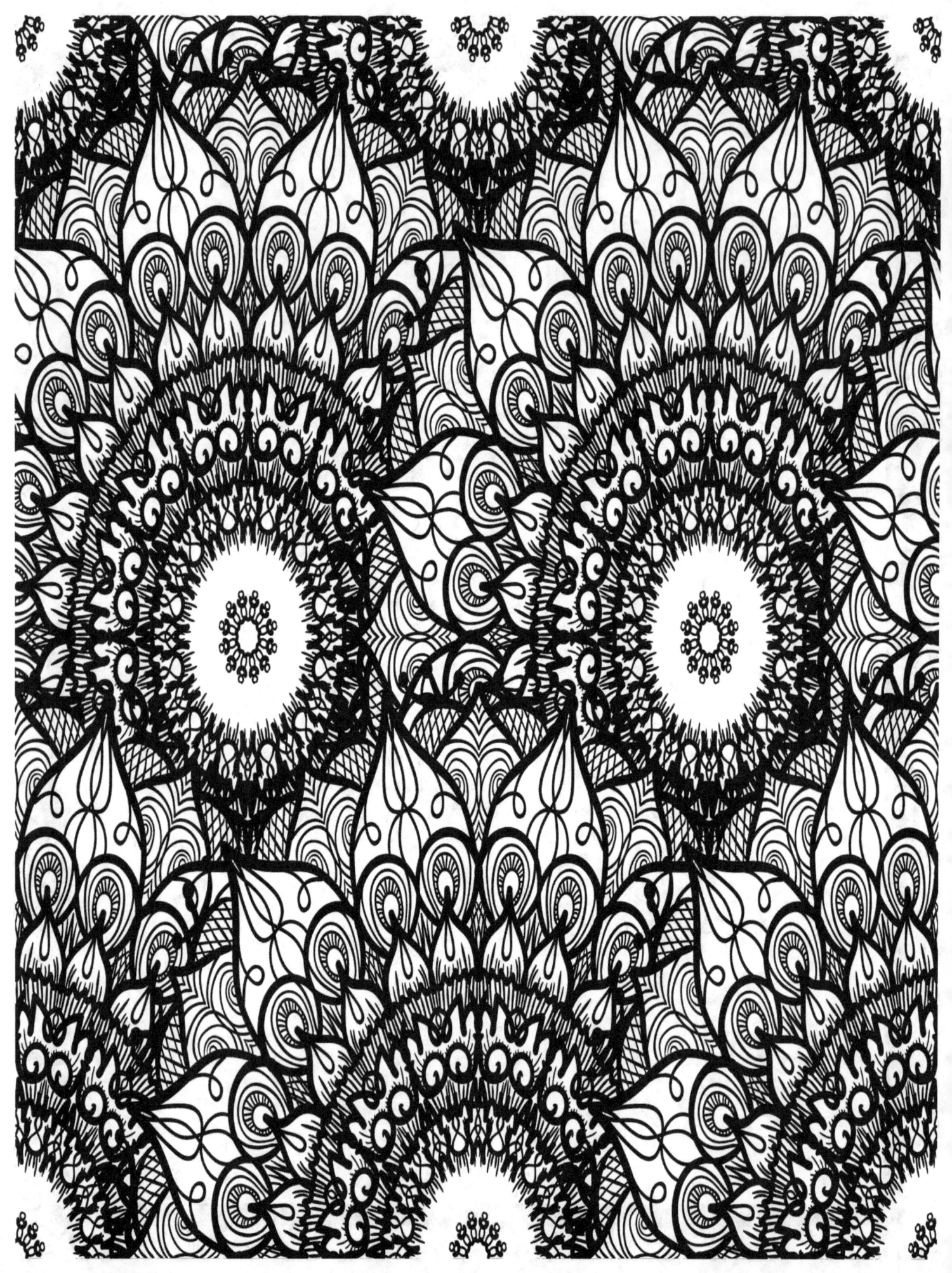

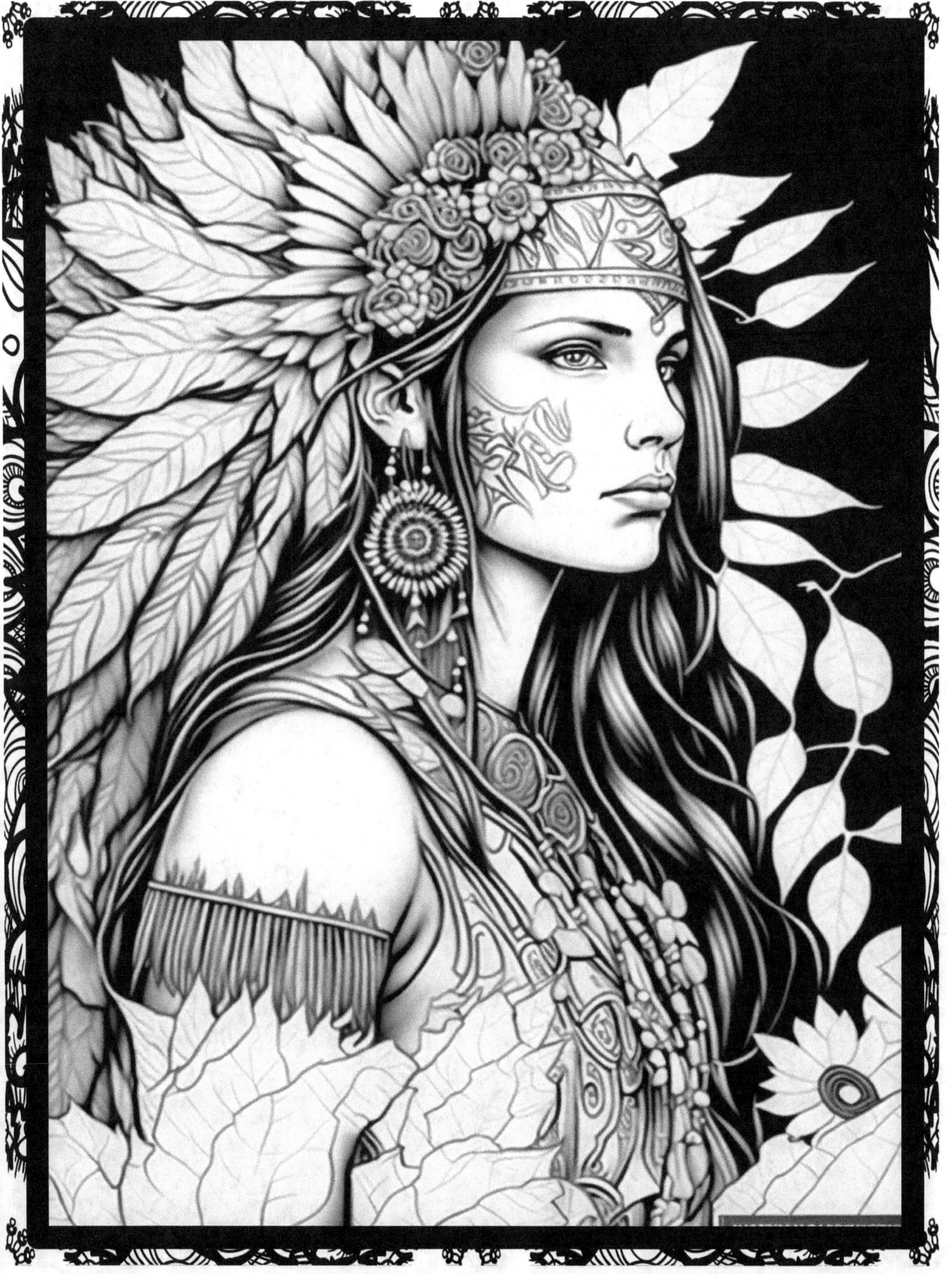

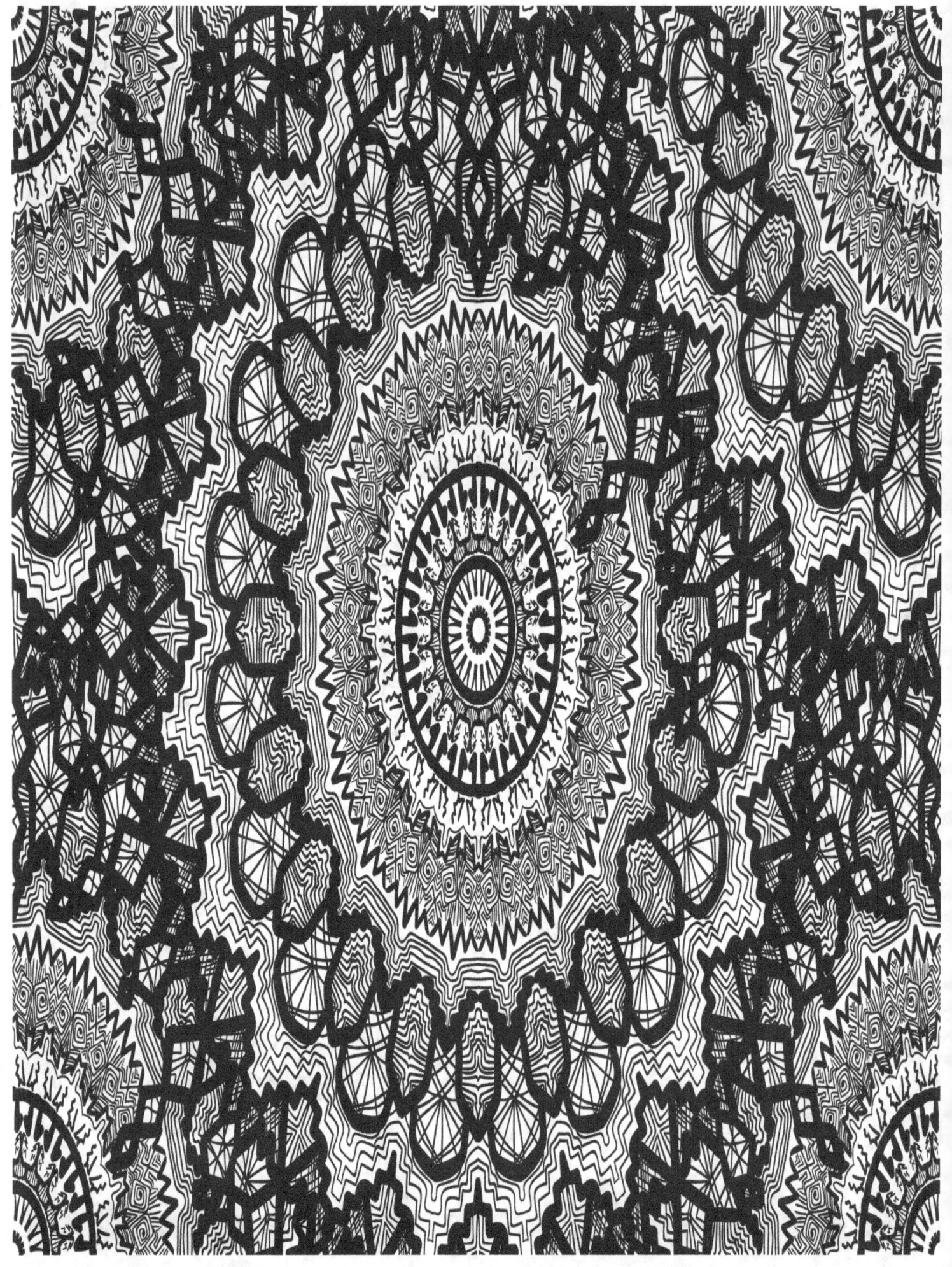

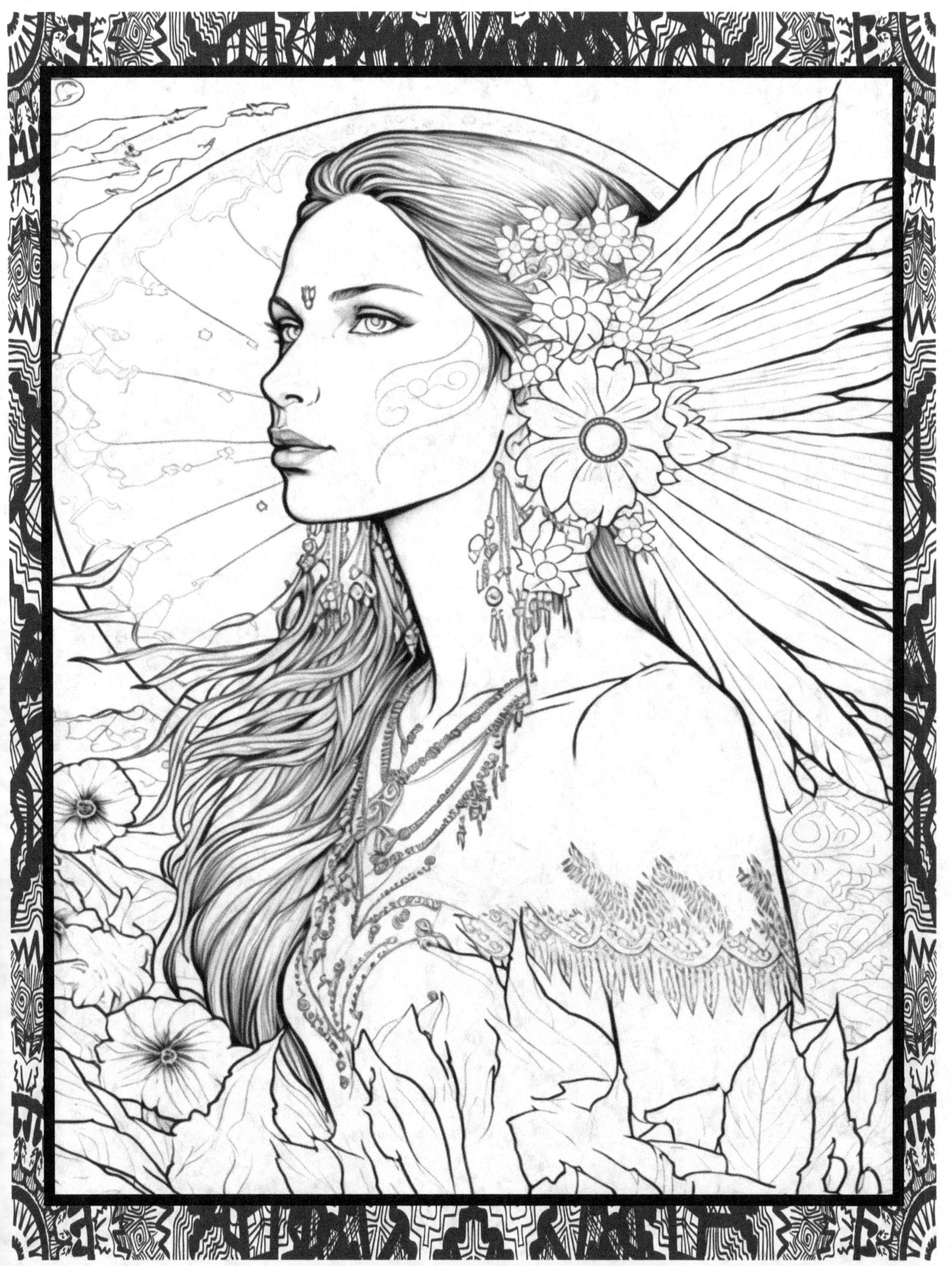

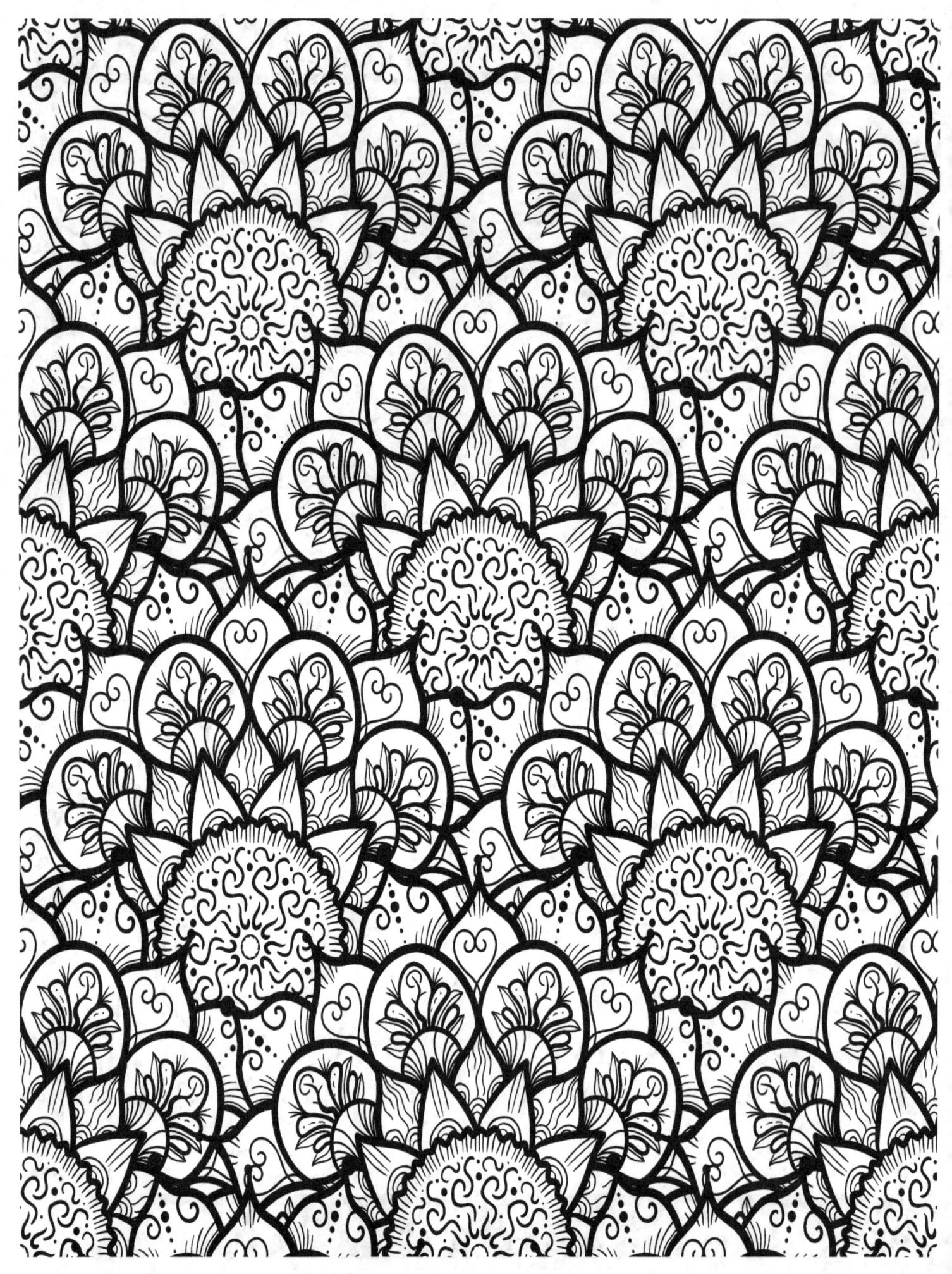

Enjoying this coloring book?

Your feedback is highly appreciated and important to me, so I would be incredibly grateful if you could take a couple of minutes to leave a quick review at the site where you purchased it.

Many thanks!

David Locatello